BLOOMSBURY
Con
Por
Wil
Guide

There are 47 individual Wildlife Trusts covering the whole of the UK and the Isle of Man and Alderney. Together The Wildlife Trusts are the largest UK voluntary organization dedicated to protecting wildlife and wild places everywhere – at land and sea. They are supported by 791,000 members, 150,000 of whom belong to their junior branch, Wildlife Watch. Every year The Wildlife Trusts work with thousands of schools, and their nature reserves and visitor centres receive millions of visitors.

The Wildlife Trusts work in partnership with hundreds of landowners and businesses in the UK. Building on their existing network of 2,250 nature reserves, The Wildlife Trusts' recovery plan for the UK's wildlife and fragmented habitats, known as A Living Landscape, is being achieved through restoring, recreating and reconnecting large areas of wildlife habitat.

The Wildlife Trusts also have a vision for the UK's seas and sea life – Living Seas, in which wildlife thrives from the depths of the oceans to the coastal shallows. In Living Seas, wildlife and habitats are recovering, the natural environment is adapting well to a changing climate, and people are inspired by marine wildlife and value the sea for the many ways in which it supports our quality of life. As well as protecting wildlife, these projects help to safeguard the ecosystems we depend on for services like clean air and water.

All 47 Wildlife Trusts are members of the Royal Society of Wildlife Trusts (Registered charity number 207238). To find your local Wildlife Trust visit wildlifetrusts.org

BLOOMSBURY

Concise
Pond
Wildlife
Guide

BLOOMSBURY
LONDON · NEW DELHI · NEW YORK · SYDNEY

Bloomsbury Natural History
An imprint of Bloomsbury Publishing Plc
50 Bedford Square, London, WC1B 3DP, UK
1385 Broadway, New York, NY 10018, USA

www.bloomsbury.com

BLOOMSBURY and the Diana logo are trademarks of Bloomsbury Publishing
Plc

First published in 2012 by New Holland Publishers (UK) Ltd
This edition published in 2015 by Bloomsbury Publishing Plc
Copyright © 2015 Bloomsbury Publishing Plc

A catalogue record for this book is available from the British Library
Library of Congress Cataloguing-in-Publication data has been applied for.
ISBN: PB: 978-1-4729-2238-0
ePDF: 978-1-4729-2240-3
ePub: 978-1-4729-2239-7

4 6 8 10 9 7 5 3

Printed and bound in China by Leo Paper Group

Contents

Introduction

The *Concise Pond Wildlife Guide* is a simple identification guide to more than 190 species of plant and animal that inhabit still-water bodies such as ponds, pools and small lakes in northern Europe. A vast number of species occurs in these habitats, so the book is selective, but it pictures and describes a good range of species that are likely to be found and identified.

Natural Wetlands

About a quarter of Britain was once covered by wetland, and large areas of the remaining land were waterlogged in winter. Ponds formed in natural dips in the landscape and river flood plains, and where springs welled up. Today, following large-scale draining of the countryside for agriculture and human habitation, only 5 per cent of the land is covered by wetlands.

In addition, many lowland rivers have been straightened, widened and deepened, and the natural meanders that would have eventually become new ponds no longer exist. Flood defences also constrain water flow and prevent the natural overflowing of rivers.

Natural ponds and wetlands generally form a mosaic with pools of different depths and sizes, some of which may dry out in summer, but will link together in winter. This allows plants and animals that may dry out in one area to recolonize elsewhere. Isolation makes this very much less likely, and a number of creatures that rely on seasonal pools, such as Tadpole and Fairy Shrimps, are now rare.

Artificial Ponds

At the same time as the land was drastically drained, ponds were created for agricultural purposes. Farms and villages all had ponds for watering livestock and irrigating crops. Mill ponds were used as reservoirs for water-powered mills. Some ponds were stocked with fish, while others were used for bathing, boating and skating. Many such ponds have been filled in, though some still remain.

Historically, many areas of fen, bog and wetland were cut by hand to provide peat for fuel. These small-scale cuttings did not completely destroy the wetlands and often created habitats suitable for wildlife; modern-day peat cutting, on the other hand, is done on a large scale with mechanical peat cutters and is likely to destroy a wetland completely. Britain's lowland raised bogs are home to many important bird species, thousands of rare insects and a wealth of unusual plants, but only a fragment of near-natural bog remains, with more than 94 per cent having been damaged or destroyed.

More recently, ponds and lakes have been created as features in retail and business parks, and on golf courses. Gravel pits are found throughout Britain, mainly in river floodplains. Small abandoned pits often flood, creating miniature wetlands. Many large excavations are deliberately flooded for recreational and conservation purposes.

Modern garden ponds became fashionable on country estates in the 18th and 19th centuries. Those of the 20th and 21st centuries are usually much less grand in scale, but now constitute about a fifth of the shallow pond habitat in England and Wales.

Man-made ponds do not wholly compensate for the loss of the natural ponds, since they tend to be deeper, have steeper sides (pond wildlife needs gentle slopes for entering and leaving the water) and permanent water, and are isolated from other water bodies.

Threats to Ponds Today

The small size and static water of ponds makes them vulnerable to pollution. On arable land, streams and ditches running through agricultural fields can pick up nutrients, silt and pesticides, which then accumulate in ponds. Although ponds can be buffered from the worst of these effects by leaving unploughed strips next to streams and ditches, the long-term solution is sustainable farming, with fertilizer and pesticide input, as well as grazing pressure, all reduced.

Shallow temporary ponds may also be deepened to prevent them from drying out, or cleared of vegetation if they are perceived to be overgrown, which can destroy the plants and kill the animals that have colonized a pond.

Garden Ponds

A good pond acts as a place where birds and mammals drink and
feed, amphibians breed, feed and sunbathe, and numerous insects
live or visit. If well sited and well designed, it is likely to seethe with
life. The size of a garden pond is not too important, though usually
the larger a pond is, the better. However, even a very small pond, only
a metre or so across, can fulfill many of the functions of a larger pond.
As general rules:

- A pond should have at least one side that slopes gently from
  the edge to the deepest point, and another area should have a
  ledge or two on which plants can be placed.
- It needs to be at least 75cm deep at the deepest point to provide a
  refuge for aquatic wildlife during extremes of weather, particularly
  in winter.
- It should be situated where it will get plenty of sunshine, and will
  not receive large quantities of leaves from nearby trees in autumn.
  Completely shaded and leaf-filled ponds have very little life,
  because the water becomes deoxygenated.
- A pond benefits from being sited next to some other rough
  habitat, at least to one side, so that animals can approach and
  leave it under cover.
- There should be a good range of plants in a pond, including
  emergent aquatics such as Arrowhead, oxygenating plants like
  Common Water-crowfoot and floating leaved plants such as water-
  lilies. A mix of plants like this helps to oxygenate the water, shades
  some parts from the sun, provides cover from predators for
  invertebrates, and gives structures for animals such as dragonflies
  and damselflies to emerge onto.
- It is possible for insects and fish to co-exist in a pond, but the
  number of insects will be kept down. If you want to have fish in
  your garden, keep them in a separate pond.

This book is an identification guide, so it does not tell you how to
actually build your pond. Consult the many how-to books and online
sources that exist for information on how to do this.

Spoonbills (*Platalea leucorodia*)
These spectacular white water birds feed on molluscs by sieving water with elegant side-to-side head movements. They breed in large reed beds in the south and the Netherlands on the Continent, wintering in western Europe and Africa. Although of European conservation concern, they have recently begun breeding in Britain again after an absence of more than 300 years. They can be seen on coastal sites in north-west and south-west England in spring or autumn, and in winter mainly on southern estuaries.

Water Dock
Rumex hydrolapathum

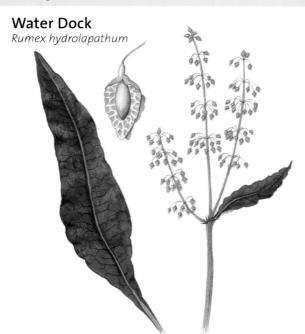

SIZE AND DESCRIPTION Much-branched perennial to 2m tall. Leaves are 80cm or more in length, tough and narrow-oval in outline. Pale green flowers are borne on tall dense spikes.

FLOWERING TIME July–September.

HABITAT AND DISTRIBUTION Wetland areas, typically growing beside lakes and rivers, and sometimes rooted in shallow and muddy water margins. Locally common in suitable habitats in lowland Europe.

Ragged-Robin
Lychnis flos-cuculi

SIZE AND DESCRIPTION
Distinctive upright
perennial to 80cm
tall. Stems are rough
and sometimes
branched. Stem leaves
are narrow, rough, grass-
like, stalkless and borne
in opposite pairs. Basal
leaves are stalked and
oblong. Flowers are pinkish-
red and ragged looking, each
with five petals that are divided into four lobes.
FLOWERING TIME May–August.
HABITAT AND DISTRIBUTION Damp places including fens, water meadows
and damp woodland rides. Widespread and locally common in
Europe; less so in the south. Has declined due to land drainage.

Marsh-marigold
Caltha palustris

SIZE AND DESCRIPTION

Striking hairless
perennial to 60cm tall,
with a creeping habit.
Basal leaves are kidney-
shaped, dark green and
borne on long stalks. Stem
leaves are smaller and more
rounded, with shorter stalks.
Flowers are 20–30mm across
and comprise five yellow
sepals but no petals; they are borne in loose clusters.

FLOWERING TIME March–July.

HABITAT AND DISTRIBUTION Marshes, wet woodlands and fens.
Widespread in most of Europe, except the Mediterranean region.

Lesser Celandine
Ranunculus ficaria

SIZE AND DESCRIPTION
Low-growing
perennial to
30cm tall, which
can form extensive
carpets. Glossy dark
green leaves are heart- or
kidney-shaped, and borne on
long stalks; they may appear
variegated. Flowers are
15–30mm across, borne on long
stems, and comprise three sepals
and 8–12 yellow petals. They open fully only in bright sunshine.
Fruits grow in rounded heads.

FLOWERING TIME March–May.

HABITAT AND DISTRIBUTION Open woodland and hedgerows. Very common
in damp and shady places. Widespread across most of Europe, and
sometimes locally abundant.

Yellow Flag
Iris pseudacorus

SIZE AND DESCRIPTION Striking perennial to 1.2m tall, with a large fleshy rhizome. Leaves are sword-shaped, bluish-green and up to 1m long. Stems are slightly flattened. Flowers are up to 10cm across, deep yellow and comprise six segments, the three outer ones being broad and long; they are borne in groups of 2–3. **FLOWERING TIME** June–July. **HABITAT AND DISTRIBUTION** Damp soils in pond and river margins, and water meadows. Widespread across most of Europe.

Meadowsweet
Filipendula ulmaria

SIZE AND DESCRIPTION Striking upright perennial to 2m tall. Leaves are
pinnately divided into pairs of large toothed leaflets, interspersed
with pairs of smaller leaflets.
Flowers are 4–6mm across with 5–6
creamy white petals; they are borne in
long frothy sprays to 25cm in length.
Small fruit is twisted spirally and
contains two seeds.
FLOWERING TIME June–September.
HABITAT AND DISTRIBUTION Damp soils
in meadows, marshes and stream
margins. Widespread across most
of Europe, but essentially absent
from the Mediterranean.

Cuckoo Flower
Cardamine pratensis

SIZE AND DESCRIPTION Attractive upright perennial to 55cm tall, with a basal rosette of pinnately divided leaves that have 1–7 pairs of rounded leaflets. Flowers are 12–20mm across with four whitish-pink or pale lilac petals; they are borne in open clusters at the stem tips. Fruits consist of narrow upright pods to 4cm long. Also called Lady's Smock.

FLOWERING TIME April–July.

HABITAT AND DISTRIBUTION Permanently damp ground in grassy areas such as meadows, fens and woodland rides. Widespread in Europe in suitable habitats.

Purple-loosestrife
Lythrum salicaria

SIZE AND DESCRIPTION
Downy perennial to
1.5m tall. Upright
stems carry narrow and
unstalked leaves either as
opposite pairs or in whorls of
three. Flowers are 10–15mm across and
borne in tight whorls, creating a tall spike; petals are reddish-purple
and there are 12 stamens. Fruit is an egg-shaped capsule.
FLOWERING TIME June–August.
HABITAT AND DISTRIBUTION Damp ground, typically beside water. Forms
extensive stands in suitable locations. Widespread across Europe.
Absent from the far north.

Marsh-mallow
Althaea officinalis

SIZE AND DESCRIPTION Densely grey-hairy perennial to 1m tall. Leaves are large, toothed and sometimes palmately lobed. Flowers are lilac-pink, with shallowly notched petals 15–20mm long; they form a tall spike.
FLOWERING TIME August–September.
HABITAT AND DISTRIBUTION Ditches, brackish marshes and banks of coastal drainage dykes. Native to Europe, North Africa and western Asia. Locally common on the southern coastal areas of Britain.

Water Forget-me-not
Myosotis scorpioides

SIZE AND DESCRIPTION Generally hairless creeping perennial to 12cm tall. Leaves are oblong to lanceolate, and borne on upright stems. Flowers are up to 8mm across, with five joined petals that are blue with a central yellow eye; they are borne in terminal clusters.

FLOWERING TIME May–September.

HABITAT AND DISTRIBUTION Watery areas on neutral and basic soils beside rivers and in marshes. Widespread in northern and central Europe.

Great Willowherb
Epilobium hirsutum

SIZE AND DESCRIPTION Downy or hairy perennial to 2m tall. Leaves are stalkless and opposite, toothed, and lanceolate to oblong. Flowers are 15–25mm across, with four pinkish-purple petals that are notched at the tips and have pale centres. Fruit capsule splits to release plumed seeds.

FLOWERING TIME June–August.

HABITAT AND DISTRIBUTION Damp soils in fens and marshes and on the margins of rivers. Often forms extensive, sizeable clumps. Widespread in most of Europe except the far north.

Water Mint
Mentha aquatica

Hairy perennial to 50cm tall, with stiff
stems, which smells strongly of mint.
Leaves are paired on the stems, oval
and toothed. Flowers are 5–8mm across,
have five petals and are pinkish-lilac;
they form rounded and dense, short-
stalked clusters at the tops of stems.
Aromatic flowers attract many insects.
Flowers in July–October. Occurs in
ditches, riverbanks, wetlands and
moorland meadows. Sometimes grows
in shallow standing water. Found
throughout Europe.

Pennyroyal
Mentha pulegium

Creeping, often mat-forming
perennial to 30cm tall. Opposite
leaves smell like Peppermint.
Flowers are small and pale lilac,
and carried in dense whorls in the
axils of the upper leaves. Flowers appear
in August–October. Found on damp
grazed ground beside ponds. Occurs in
much of Europe and North Africa. Scarce
in Britain; found in scattered localities in
southern England and Ireland, Wales
and the Channel Islands.

Lords-and-ladies
Arum maculatum

SIZE AND DESCRIPTION Upright and
hairless perennial to 25cm tall. Leaves
are arrowhead-shaped, long-stalked, shiny
green and sometimes purple-spotted;
they appear before the flowers, in early
spring. Flowers are borne on a spike,
with the male flowers above the
female ones; both are hidden at
the base of the yellow-green spathe
and below the purple-brown cylindrical spadix.
Ripe berries are bright red and appear in autumn.
FLOWERING TIME April–May.
HABITAT AND DISTRIBUTION Woodland and shady hedgerows, usually on
damp soils. Widespread in western, central and southern Europe.

HOW THE PLANT IS POLLINATED

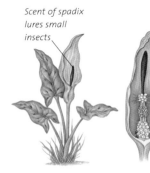

Scent of spadix
lures small
insects

Insects move down
past backwards-
pointing hairs,
which trap them

Insects move between
male and female
flower clusters;
pollinating flowers;
they escape when
hairs wither and wilt

Common Figwort
Scrophularia nodosa

SIZE AND DESCRIPTION Hairless
perennial to 70cm tall, which is
foetid smelling when rubbed.
Stems are square in cross-
section. Leaves are short-stalked,
oval and pointed, with sharp-
toothed margins. Flowers are
7–10mm across, two-lipped and
green with maroon-brown lips; they
are borne in open, branched spikes.
FLOWERING TIME June–September.
HABITAT AND DISTRIBUTION Damp
woodland, and shady verges and
hedgerows. Widespread in central,
western and southern Europe.

Bugle
Ajuga reptans

SIZE AND DESCRIPTION Upright perennial to 20cm tall, with hairy stems and leafy creeping runners that root at intervals. Leaves are blunt, sometimes toothed and often stalked; the lower leaves form a rosette and the stem leaves are paired. Flowers are 15mm long and bluish-violet, with five petals forming a tube.

FLOWERING TIME May–July.

HABITAT AND DISTRIBUTION Woods and grassy places, usually on damp heavy soils. Found almost everywhere in Europe.

Marsh Lousewort
Pedicularis palustris

SIZE AND DESCRIPTION Spreading perennial to 60cm tall, which is branched from the base. A semi-parasite of wetland plants. Leaves are alternate and feathery, varying from roughly triangular or lanceolate to pinnately lobed and toothed. Flowers are 20–25mm long, pink and two-lipped, with a straight corolla. Fruits consist of inflated capsules.

FLOWERING TIME April–July.

HABITAT AND DISTRIBUTION Damp heaths and moors on nutrient-poor acid soils. Widespread but local in western and central Europe.

Brooklime
Veronica beccabunga

SIZE AND DESCRIPTION Hairless perennial to 30cm tall, with creeping and rooting stems that become upright. Leaves are oval and fleshy, and borne on short stalks. Flowers are 7–8mm across and blue with white centres; they are borne in pairs arising from the leaf axils.

FLOWERING TIME May–September.

HABITAT AND DISTRIBUTION
Shallow water and damp soil beside ponds and rivers. Widespread in suitable habitats across Europe, except the far north and drier Mediterranean regions.

Bog-myrtle
Myrica gale

Size and description Woody, brown-stemmed shrub to 2m tall. Leaves are oval and grey-green, with a resinous fragrance. Ovoid orange male catkins and pendulous brown female catkins grow on separate plants. Fruits consist of brownish nuts.

Flowering time April.

Habitat and distribution Characteristic of boggy habitats, usually on acid soils, including bogs, heathland and fens. Widespread but local.

Common Valerian
Valeriana officinalis

SIZE AND DESCRIPTION Upright perennial to 1.5m tall, with flowering
stems growing from the base. Leaves are spear-shaped, often toothed
and paired. Flowers are 3–5mm long, each with five pinkish-lilac
petals forming a tube; they are borne in broad, tightly packed and
branched heads. Fruits are oblong, and bear a feathery parachute.

FLOWERING TIME June–August.

HABITAT AND DISTRIBUTION Damp meadows, riverbanks, ditches, damp
forests, fens and scrub. Found almost everywhere in Europe.

Hemp-agrimony
Eupatorium cannabinum

SIZE AND DESCRIPTION Distinctive upright downy perennial to 1.75m tall.
Stems are often reddish. Leaves are divided into 3–5 lobes, and borne
in opposite pairs up the stems. Flowers are dull pink and small; they
are grouped in dense clusters 2–5mm across, which are borne in loose
terminal inflorescences.

FLOWERING TIME July–September.

HABITAT AND DISTRIBUTION Damp ground such as fens and marshes;
occasionally drier situations. Widespread in suitable habitats across
most of Europe except the far north.

Common Duckweed
Lemna minor

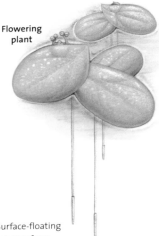

Fruiting plant

Flowering plant

SIZE AND DESCRIPTION Surface-floating
aquatic perennial that may form
a green carpet over the surface of
ponds, lakes and canals by late summer. Leaves are to 5mm across,
round and flat, with a dangling root that hangs down into the water.
Flowers are inconspicuous, minute and borne in hollows on the
surfaces of the leaves. Other species of duckweed found in Britain
include Fat Duckweed (*Lemna gibba*), Ivy-leaved Duckweed (*L. trisulca*),
Least Duckweed (*L. minuta*) and Greater Duckweed (*Spirodela
polyrhiza*). All are fast growing and can be invasive.
FLOWERING TIME June–July.
HABITAT AND DISTRIBUTION Ponds, lakes and canals. Common and
widespread throughout Europe.

Broad-leaved Pondweed
Potamogeton natans

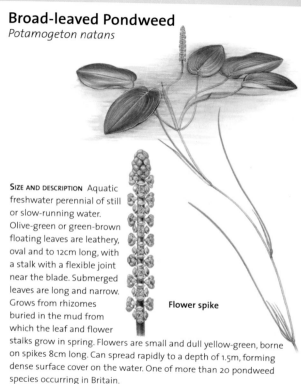

SIZE AND DESCRIPTION Aquatic freshwater perennial of still or slow-running water. Olive-green or green-brown floating leaves are leathery, oval and to 12cm long, with a stalk with a flexible joint near the blade. Submerged leaves are long and narrow. Grows from rhizomes buried in the mud from which the leaf and flower stalks grow in spring. Flowers are small and dull yellow-green, borne on spikes 8cm long. Can spread rapidly to a depth of 1.5m, forming dense surface cover on the water. One of more than 20 pondweed species occurring in Britain.

Flower spike

FLOWERING TIME May–September.

HABITAT AND DISTRIBUTION Still or slow-flowing water bodies. Common and widespread throughout Europe.

Common Water-crowfoot
Ranunculus aquatilis

SIZE AND DESCRIPTION Attractive annual or perennial to 1m long; by the end of summer it may blanket the surface of the wetland habitats where it grows. Surface leaves are rounded and toothed, while submerged ones are finely divided and thread-like. Flowers are 12–20mm across, with five white petals. Fruits grow in rounded heads.

FLOWERING TIME April–August.

HABITAT AND DISTRIBUTION Still waters, and slow-flowing streams and rivers. Widespread throughout most of lowland Europe.

Bogbean
Menyanthes trifoliata

Distinctive aquatic perennial to 30cm tall. Leaves are divided into groups of three leaflets and held above the water's surface. Flowers are pink and white with fringed petals, borne on leafless spikes up to 30cm long. Flowers appear in May–July. Grows in still water in silty ponds, small lakes, marshes, fens and bogs. Widespread and common across most of the temperate northern hemisphere; rare in the Mediterranean.

Arrowhead
Sagittaria sagittifolia

Upright and hairless aquatic perennial to 90cm tall. Aerial leaves are shaped like arrowheads and borne on long upright stalks. Plant also has floating and submerged leaves. Flowers are 15–20mm across with three white petals, each with a purple spot at the base; they are borne in whorls. Flowers in July–August. Found in still or slow-moving waters. Widespread in most of Europe, except the far north and Mediterranean.

Yellow Water-lily
Nuphar lutea

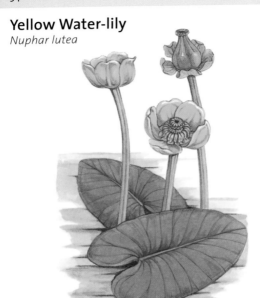

SIZE AND DESCRIPTION Striking aquatic perennial with oval, leathery floating leaves that are heart-shaped at the bases and up to 40cm across. It also has thinner, wavy-edged submerged leaves. Flowers are up to 60mm across with overlapping yellow sepals hiding the petals; they are borne on slender stalks above the water.

FLOWERING TIME June–September.

HABITAT AND DISTRIBUTION Still or slow-flowing, nutrient-rich water. Forms extensive carpets over the water's surface in suitable locations. Widespread across lowland Europe in suitable habitats.

White Water-lily
Nymphaea alba

SIZE AND DESCRIPTION Floating plant growing in still or slow-flowing fresh water to a depth of 3m. Leaves are 10–30cm across and rounded. Floating flowers are 15–20cm across, cup-shaped and fragrant. Their 20–25 white or pinkish-white petals open fully only in bright sunshine. Fruits are globular, green and warty, splitting underwater to release many floating seeds.

FLOWERING TIME June–August.

HABITAT AND DISTRIBUTION Ponds and lakes. Widespread and locally common in lowland Europe in suitable habitats.

Fringed Water-lily
Nymphoides peltata

SIZE AND DESCRIPTION Aquatic perennial somewhat similar to Yellow Water-lily (page 34), but smaller and with completely different flowers. Leaves are 3–8cm across, floating, and rounded or kidney-shaped. Flowers are yellow, fringed and inconspicuous, growing in leafy spikes with tiny bracts.

FLOWERING TIME June–September.

HABITAT AND DISTRIBUTION Shallow, slow-moving water in ponds, lakes, drains, dykes and canals. Found in most of Europe; locally common in southern England and naturalized elsewhere.

Greater Bladderwort
Utricularia vulgaris

SIZE AND DESCRIPTION Carnivorous aquatic plant with submerged stems to 1m long, and leafless flowering stems rising up to 20cm above the water. Small bladders along the submerged stems trap tiny invertebrates. Leaves are finely divided, with bristled teeth. Flowers are 12–18mm long and deep yellow; they are borne in clusters on stems. Globular capsule splits to release many angular seeds.
FLOWERING TIME July–August.
HABITAT AND DISTRIBUTION Ponds, lakes and ditches. Occurs throughout Europe.

Water Plantain
Alisma plantago-aquatica

SIZE AND DESCRIPTION Aquatic and
emergent perennial to 1m tall,
forming a leafy tuft with upright
flowering stems. Leaves are oval
or spear-shaped with a pointed
blade. Flowers are pale lilac or white,
8–10mm across and form a head
with branches.
FLOWERING TIME June–August.
HABITAT AND DISTRIBUTION Edges and shallows
of ponds, lakes, rivers and canals. Found
throughout Europe in suitable locations.

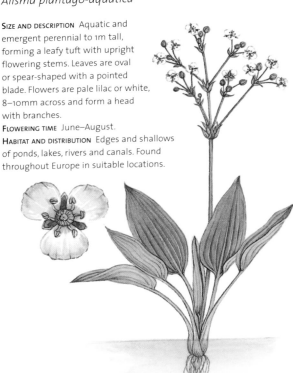

Bulrush
Typha latifolia

SIZE AND DESCRIPTION Aquatic or semi-aquatic
rhizomatous perennial to 3m tall. Leaves are
grey-green and 8–25mm wide. Flowers are
borne in spikes comprising a sausage-
like brown array of female flowers,
and a narrow terminal spire of
male flowers above this. Also
called Reedmace.
FLOWERING TIME June–July.
HABITAT AND DISTRIBUTION Shallow water or
bare mud at the margins of ponds, pools,
lakes, canals, ditches and slow-running
rivers. Found Europe-wide, including in
Britain, though scarce in Scotland.

Common Reed
Phragmites australis

SIZE AND DESCRIPTION Robust rhizomatous perennial; the tallest British grass. Leaves are greyish-green and 10–30mm wide. Produces large and many-branched purplish panicles to 40cm tall, which become paler with age.

FLOWERING TIME August–October.

HABITAT AND DISTRIBUTION Forms extensive dense stands in the shallow water of ponds, lakes, broads, fens, ditches and estuaries. Found throughout Europe.

Spaghnum moss
Spaghnum spp.

Description The peat-forming mosses are unique plants that grow from the top, laying down new growth in the form of leaves and stems, and leaving behind the dead growth, which continues to hold water long after life has passed. The growing tip of the plant is vibrant green, orange or red, depending on the species. Working down the plant, it breaks down slowly, giving way to whites and yellows, and at the bottom becoming rich brown. Deep below the surface, the leaves distintegrate, still holding water; the black ooze under a moss clump is the start of the formation of peat.

Habitat and distribution Forms raised bogs in lowland areas and blanket bogs on moorland. Occurs mainly in the northern hemisphere. Bog pools are part terrestrial and part aquatic, and harbour interesting animal communities that include dragonflies, water beetles, pond skaters and water boatmen.

Trees and Ponds

Trees can offer shelter and shade for animals associated with ponds, and help slow down the growth of algae, which thrives in full sun. The trees shown here are those that thrive near water, such as willows, poplars and alders; also included are examples of suitable small trees that can be grown near garden ponds. The latter should be chosen and sited with care to avoid too much shade being thrown onto the pond, prevent damage to the pond liner by tree roots and minimize the amount of fallen leaf drop on to the pond in autumn. Very thirsty trees with deep roots, such as poplars, should be avoided since they can cause the soil around a pond to dry out.

Common Osier *Salix viminalis* Height to 10m. Deciduous tree with a narrow and upright crown. Leaves are narrow, lance-shaped and tapering, with dull green uppersides and silver-grey beneath. Catkins are erect, and male flowers have yellow anthers. Fruit is flask-shaped. Prefers damp places.

White Willow *Salix alba* Height to 30m. Deciduous. Mature crown is domed, with ascending branches. Leaves are lance-shaped and shiny, with grey-green uppersides and almost white undersides. Pale yellow catkins. Fluffy seeds are formed on female catkins. Favours damp soil, particularly near ponds and rivers.

Goat Willow *Salix caprea* Height to 20m. Deciduous tree with a domed crown. Leaves are egg-shaped, broader towards the bases and dark to grey-green. Female catkins are green, male catkins silver-grey tinged with yellow. Fruits have many woolly seeds on female catkins ('pussy willows'). Grows in damp and dry woods and scrub.

Crack Willow *Salix fragilis* Height to 20m. Deciduous tree with a cone-shaped crown when young, becoming broad and rounded in maturity. Leaves are lance-shaped with shiny green uppersides, and bluish-white underneath. Twigs readily break and root easily. Male catkins are pale yellow, female catkins green. Woolly white seeds form on female catkins. Grows in damp lowland woodland, and along the banks of rivers and canals.

Bay Willow *Salix pentandra* Height to 20m. Deciduous. Highly glossy leaves and twigs give a varnished look to this small tree or shrub. Leaves are elliptical to lance-shaped, leathery, and dark above, paler beneath. Dense male catkins are pale yellow, female catkins shorter and greenish. Seeds are silky and plumed. Grows in waterways and wet soils.

Grey Poplar *Populus x canescens*

Height to 40m. Deciduous tree with a columnar and open crown. Leaves are placed alternately, vary considerably in shape and have white undersides. Suckers readily grow from the roots. Male catkins are green, female catkins have a golden tinge. Grows on damp ground, near rivers and in water meadows.

Common Alder *Alnus glutinosa*

Height to 25m. Deciduous tree with a broad-domed or conical crown. Leaves are rounded and alternate. Male and female catkins grow on the same tree. Buds are stacked with green fruits, ripening in spring. Female cones turn black and woody, and stay on the tree all winter. Thrives in wet ground, lining the banks of rivers and streams.

Alder Buckthorn *Frangula alnus*

Height to 6m. Deciduous shrub or small tree with a rounded crown with several stems. Leaves are oval, tapered and have wavy margins. Small flower clusters are formed in the leaf axils. Fruits are globe-shaped and berry-like, ripening from green, then yellow to purplish-black. Grows in hedgerows and understorey in moist woodland.

Silver Birch *Betula pendula*
Height to 30m. Deciduous tree with a
slender habit; pointed crown when
young and domed when mature.
Leaves are alternate on slender, hairless
stalks, triangular, pointed and with
toothed margins. Male and female
flowers grow in separate drooping
catkins on the same tree. They break
up into winged windborne seeds in
winter. Base is often rich in fungi.

Crab Apple *Malus sylvestris*
Height to 9m. Deciduous spreading
tree with dense foliage. Leaves are
oval to egg-shaped, wider near the
tips, with serrated edges. Flowers
have white or pink petals. Fruit is
globe-shaped, like a small apple, and
greenish. Widespread, favouring old
woodland and hedgerows.

Hawthorn *Crataegus monogyna*
Height to 16m. Deciduous tree with
a rounded crown, dense branches
and twigs bearing numerous sharp
thorns. Leaves have 2–3 pairs of lobes;
they are shiny green and turn yellow
or red in autumn. Bears clusters of
creamy-white flowers. Fruit is a small
dark red berry with one seed. Widely
used as a hedging shrub, and also as
a standard in woodland.

Pond Sponge
Spongilla lacustris

SIZE AND DESCRIPTION Usually erect, creamy-white or green freshwater sponge with finger-like branches 2–10mm thick. Surface is uneven and roughened by tiny spines.

HABITAT AND DISTRIBUTION Ponds, lakes and slow-flowing streams throughout Europe.

FOOD AND HABITS A filter-feeder like all sponges, straining minute organisms such as protozoa and bacteria from the water as it flows through its cavities. Attaches itself to submerged underwater objects such as boulders, rocks, logs and tree roots.

Green Hydra
Hydra viridissima

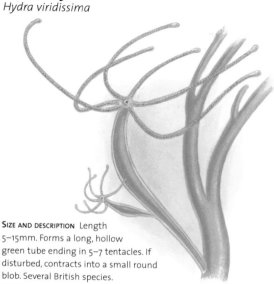

SIZE AND DESCRIPTION Length
5–15mm. Forms a long, hollow
green tube ending in 5–7 tentacles. If
disturbed, contracts into a small round
blob. Several British species.

HABITAT AND DISTRIBUTION Widespread and common in small, clean and
weedy ponds, ditches and lakes.

FOOD AND HABITS Normally attached to the stems and leaves of water
plants. Uses the adhesive stinging cells on its tentacles to transfer
prey, consisting mainly of crustaceans like water fleas, to its body
cavity for digestion. Hydras are not always attached to the substrate
and can move from one spot to another, either by gliding along on
the basal disc or by somersaulting to a different attachment point.
They are related to jellyfish.

Flatworm
Dugesia tigrina

SIZE AND DESCRIPTION Length to 3cm, but very variable. Mottled grey-brown with a paler underside. Single pair of eyes. One of about 10 flatworm species found in Britain, including *Polycelis nigra*, which is black, about 10mm long and commonly found in ponds.

HABITAT AND DISTRIBUTION Undersides of stones and leaves. American species often found in garden ponds, into which it was accidentally introduced with ornamental fish.

FOOD AND HABITS Feeds on a wide range of invertebrates. Usually reproduces asexually. Sometimes seen crawling rapidly on the bottom mud, or even on the underside of the surface film.

Sludge Worm
Tubifex tubifex

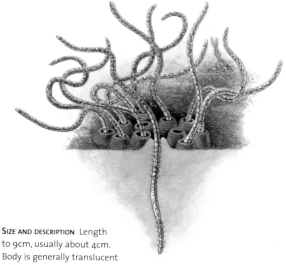

SIZE AND DESCRIPTION Length
to 9cm, usually about 4cm.
Body is generally translucent
red. Unable to swim, and lives buried in mud.
HABITAT AND DISTRIBUTION Often abundant in muddy substrates,
especially where the organic content is high, for example in areas of
sewage pollution. Widely distributed in Britain.
FOOD AND HABITS Lives head down in a vertical burrow cemented with
slime, in sand or mud. The protruding tail is used to gain oxygen, and
food in the form of suspended decaying organic matter, from the
water current.

Water bear
Echiniscus trisetasus

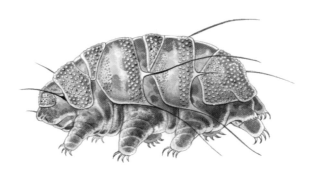

Size and description Length less than 1mm. Tiny animal with a stout body and four pairs of stubby legs ending in four single claws. Cuticle has a hard plate on the dorsal surface. Bear-like gait, which gives this group of animals its common name. There are many species in this genus, and also other genera of water bear. They are difficult to identify correctly, with the claw structure being key in identification.
Habitat and distribution Damp vegetation at the edge of fresh water, among mosses and liverworts and the detritus of ponds and lakes.
Food and habits Feeds by sucking the contents from plant cells. Lifespan 3–30 months.

Medicinal Leech
Hirudo medicinalis

SIZE AND DESCRIPTION Length to 20cm. Stout leech with ten eyes in two longitudinal rows. Upper surface is dark olive with orange-red longitudinal lines; underside is grey or light grey-olive; black-bordered pale yellow line along each side. Anterior sucker is indistinct.

HABITAT AND DISTRIBUTION Once common and widespread in marshy pools and fens, but now scarce, mainly due to habitat drainage. Thought to occur in about 20 scattered locations in Britain, and extinct in Ireland. In Europe legally protected in most of its range, including Britain.

FOOD AND HABITS Feeds by sucking blood from mammals, amphibians and fish, possessing teeth that can bite through human skin – it is the only British leech species that has the ability to do this.

Horse Leech
Haemopis sanguisuga

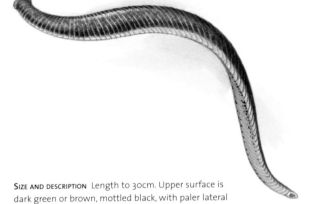

SIZE AND DESCRIPTION Length to 30cm. Upper surface is
dark green or brown, mottled black, with paler lateral
stripes. One of about 15 leech species in Britain.

HABITAT AND DISTRIBUTION Widespread but quite scarce, and found
mainly in shallow weedy pools.

FOOD AND HABITS Ingests small invertebrates and carrion, and sucks
body fluids from large molluscs. The rear sucker of a leech is used to
fix it in place. Both suckers are used for locomotion: it can crawl like a
caterpillar by arching its back and using the front and back suckers to
push and pull. Leeches can also swim by employing an undulating
movement of the body.

Great Ram's-horn Snail
Planorbis corneus

SIZE AND DESCRIPTION Shell diameter to 3.5cm; height to 1.2cm. The shape of the dark brown shell gives this large snail its common name. One of more than 50 snail species found in Britain.

HABITAT AND DISTRIBUTION Ponds, lakes and slow-flowing rivers. Also found in garden ponds because it is sold by aquarium dealers. Native range is from Europe to central Asia.

FOOD AND HABITS Feeds on algae on stones and plants. Its eggs, which are laid on stones, may be spread to other ponds whenever they stick to the feet of birds.

Great Pond Snail
Lymnaea stagnalis

SIZE AND DESCRIPTION Shell height to 5cm; width to 2.5cm. Pointed spiral shell is yellowish to dark brown.

HABITAT AND DISTRIBUTION Large, calcium-rich ponds, ditches, lakes and slow-flowing rivers and canals. The most common water snail in areas of hard water. Widely distributed across Europe, and common in many countries.

FOOD AND HABITS Feeds on algae and decaying vegetation. Eggs are laid in a sausage-shaped gelatinous sac on the undersides of leaves.

Ear Pond Snail
Lymnaea auricularia

SIZE AND DESCRIPTION Shell height to 3cm; width to 2.5cm. Shiny, rounded shell that is yellow, beige or tan. Ear-shaped aperture is very large and occupies four-fifths of the shell's entire length.

HABITAT AND DISTRIBUTION Freshwater ponds, lakes and slow-flowing, muddy-bottomed rivers. Native to Europe and Asia.

FOOD AND HABITS Feeds on detritus and algae attached to water plants or stones. Like the other snails described here, a pulmonate (belonging to a terrestrial snail group that has adopted an aquatic life), able to breathe atmospheric air by means of a 'lung'. All pulmonate snails are hermaphrodite and capable of laying eggs.

Moss Bladder Snail

Aplxa hypnorum

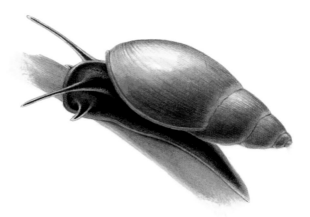

SIZE AND DESCRIPTION Shell length to 1.3cm. Translucent, pale brown, thin and shiny shell that is sinistral, or left-handed, and elongated with a narrow aperture. Soft parts are black or dark grey, contrasting with the shell.

HABITAT AND DISTRIBUTION Ponds and ditches, especially those that dry out periodically, in northern and central Europe.

FOOD AND HABITS Feeds on detritus. Adult snails die when a temporary pond dries out, but the eggs are very resistant to drying out.

Orb-shell Cockle
Sphaerium corneum

SIZE AND DESCRIPTION Length to 1.1cm. Very small freshwater clam. Small, round, lustrous yellowish-brown shell. Several species in Europe; this is one of the largest.

HABITAT AND DISTRIBUTION Common in ponds and streams. Widespread in Britain and other parts of northern and central Europe.

FOOD AND HABITS Suspension feeder, filtering food particles from the water, which is drawn in and expelled through two siphons. Young individuals can climb quickly through vegetation, while older ones tend to burrow in the mud or sand at the bottom. Hermaphrodite, producing about six fully developed young at a time. Life-span of about three years.

Swan Mussel
Anodonta cygnea

Size and description Shell length to 23cm. The largest bivalve in British waters. Yellowish-green to olive-brown shell, elongated oval in shape with a sharply angled posterior end. Surface is marked by distinct growth lines.

Habitat and distribution Common in large, mud-bottomed ponds, lakes, canals and slow-flowing rivers.

Food and habits Front part of the shell normally lies buried, but the siphons at the posterior end are always exposed. They are used by the mussel to breathe, and to feed on small animals and algae. Long life-span of 11 years or more.

Painter's Mussel
Unio pictorum

SIZE AND DESCRIPTION Shell length to 10cm. Shell is buff or light brown.
HABITAT AND DISTRIBUTION Large, mud-bottomed ponds, lakes, canals
and rivers in northern and central Europe.
FOOD AND HABITS Filter feeder, using two siphons to suck in food
particles and oxygen in water, and to expel waste materials. The
shell is normally partly buried, with the siphons exposed. It was
historically used as a conveniently sized and shaped receptacle
for holding artist's paint. Life-span of 10 years or more. The concentric
lines on the shells of mussels can be used to determine the ages
of the animals.

Water Hog-louse
Ascellus aquaticus

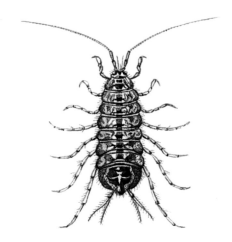

SIZE AND DESCRIPTION Length to 1.5cm. Grey-brown body that is flattened dorso-ventrally. Seven pairs of walking legs. Very recognizable because it is the closest living relative of woodlice.

HABITAT AND DISTRIBUTION Widespread and abundant in small stagnant ponds; also found along canal margins and in sluggish streams with weeds and leaf litter.

FOOD AND HABITS Like woodlice it is a recycler, grubbing around in weeds and dead plant matter at the bottoms of ponds. Female lays eggs in April–May, then carries them around in her marsupium (pouch). Young remain in the pouch for a while even after hatching.

Cyclops
Cyclops sp.

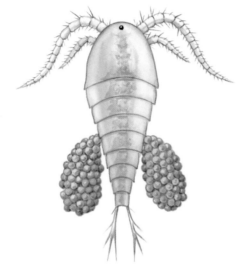

SIZE AND DESCRIPTION Length to 3mm. Pear-shaped body ending in a forked tail. Single eye and long antennules (first antennae). Around 40 species in Britain, all of which are very similar.

HABITAT AND DISTRIBUTION Widespread in all kinds of freshwater body apart from the most polluted.

FOOD AND HABITS Feeds on food particles suspended in water, and on dead animals. Two egg sacs are carried by the female on her side, like large panniers (as shown here). Lives for a year or less.

Water Flea
Daphne pulex

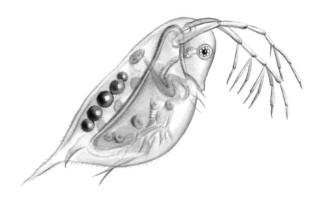

SIZE AND DESCRIPTION Length to 5mm. Swims using second pair of antennae (smaller first pair is sensory).
HABITAT AND DISTRIBUTION Shallow weedy ponds, lake edges and debris in still fresh water. Can be abundant, with 'blooms' giving water a red-brown tinge.
FOOD AND HABITS Filters food particles from water. Lives from a few weeks to six months.

Tadpole Shrimp
Triops cancriformis

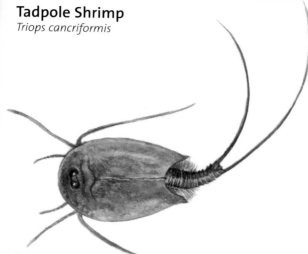

SIZE AND DESCRIPTION
Length to 11cm. Broad, oval
carapace concealing the front part of the body, two long, tapering
tails and up to 70 pairs of limbs. An ancient species that is virtually
the same today as it was more than 200 million years ago.

HABITAT AND DISTRIBUTION
Seasonally flooded ponds that dry out in
summer. Rare and endangered in many parts of Europe, including
Britain, where it is known from a few populations in Scotland, and
one in a pond in the New Forest, England.

FOOD AND HABITS
Eats small aquatic invertebrates and plants, and tiny
particles extracted from sediment. Adapted to living in temporary
water pools. Adults die when the water dries up, leaving behind eggs
that can be dormant for years until wet conditions return.

Freshwater Shrimp
Gammarus lacustris

SIZE AND DESCRIPTION Length to 2.5cm. Drab olive, grey-brown or red-brown body that is curved. Antennules are only slightly longer than the antennae. Swims on its side.

HABITAT AND DISTRIBUTION Widespread and often abundant in lakes across northern Britain, Ireland and northern Germany northwards, and also found in ponds.

FOOD AND HABITS Scavenges in water, performing the same function as woodlice do above the surface.

Fairy Shrimp
Chirocephalus diaphanous

SIZE AND DESCRIPTION Length to 2.5cm. Translucent animal with black eyes, and reddened tips to the abdomen and appendages. Thorax is made up of 12 body segments, and there are 11 pairs of limbs and two pairs of antennae.

HABITAT AND DISTRIBUTION Temporary pools, preferring sites with regular disturbance, for instance from livestock. Found across much of Europe except the far north. Under threat due to habitat destruction, and protected in Britain.

FOOD AND HABITS Filter-feeder, eating zooplankton and detritus. Usually swims on its back. Its eggs require a period of drying out. The lifecycle of the species is very fast, perhaps around three months long.

Water Springtail
Podura aquatica

Size and description Length to 1.5mm. Generally bluish-grey, but sometimes almost black.

Habitat and distribution Fairly common and often abundant on different still-water types, with a Holarctic distribution.

Food and habits Scavenges mainly for vegetable matter on the surface of all kinds of still water. When disturbed, able to jump several centimetres up into the air without breaking the water's surface tension. Large numbers of springtails may bunch into groups, appearing like a puff of soot on the surface of the water.

Springtail
Sminthurides aquaticus

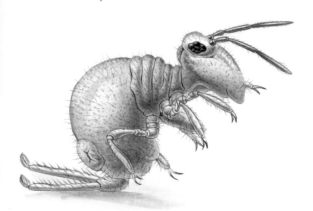

SIZE AND DESCRIPTION Length to 1mm (f). Males are about half the size of females. Globular body that is yellow with some bluish pigment on the upper surface. Springtails are named for the spring-like mechanism (furcula) on the underside of the abdomen. When at rest, this is folded forwards and held under tension with a clasp-like structure. When this is released, a springtail can jump a distance many times its own length.

HABITAT AND DISTRIBUTION Most frequently the surface of standing water. Common and widely distributed in Britain and other parts of Europe.

FOOD AND HABITS Feeds on decaying vegetation, algae and other materials. Springtail life stages include egg, nymph and adult, with little difference between immature and adult forms.

Pond Olive
Cloeon dipterum

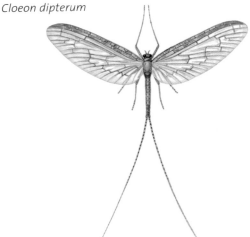

SIZE AND DESCRIPTION Length 7–11mm (body); 12–18mm (tails). Delicate insect with two tails, although many mayfly species have three tails. Also unlike other mayflies, which have two pairs of wings, the front of which are the largest, it has only one pair. Front edges of female's wings are brownish, while male has big eyes that are located higher than the rest of his head.

HABITAT AND DISTRIBUTION Small areas of still water. Common in Britain and other parts of Europe.

FOOD AND HABITS Flies May–October. Mostly active at dawn and dusk, or at night. Adult mayflies do not feed, living only for a maximum of a few days, with some species living for less than an hour. Nymphs feed on algae.

Azure Damselfly
Coenagrion puella

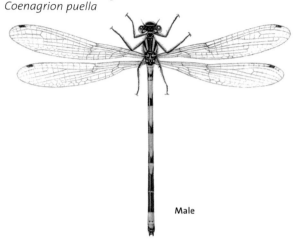

Male

SIZE AND DESCRIPTION Length 33–35mm; hindwing 15–24mm. Male has a blue abdomen with black markings and a totally blue eighth segment. Female has a dark abdomen with blue or green markings.

HABITAT AND DISTRIBUTION Prefers small sheltered ponds, including garden ponds, with emergent vegetation. Found from Ireland and southern Scotland across Europe, and south to North Africa. One of the most common damselflies.

FOOD AND HABITS Flies mid-May–late August. Often seen in sunny meadows. Adults feed on small flying insects. Nymphs feed on small aquatic crustaceans and insects.

Common Blue Damselfly
Enallagama cyathigerum

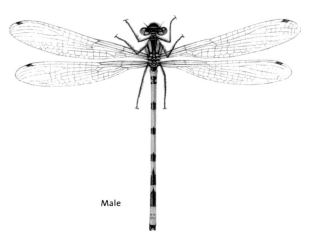

Male

SIZE AND DESCRIPTION Length 29–36mm; hindwing 15–21mm. Male has a blue abdomen with black markings; segments 8–9 are all-blue. Female has a yellowish or bluish abdomen with variable dark markings.

HABITAT AND DISTRIBUTION Variety of inland water bodies, including ponds, gravel pits, lakes, slow rivers and canals, throughout Europe except the far north and south. One of the most common dragonflies.

FOOD AND HABITS Flies May–September. Feeds on insects such as aphids. May pounce on dark spots on leaves, mistaking them for insects. Strong flier. Sometimes occurs in clusters of hundreds of individuals.

Large Red Damselfly
Pyrrhosoma nymphula

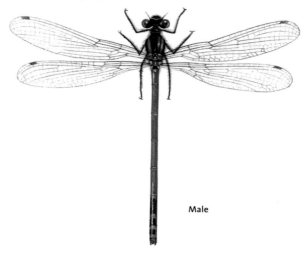

Male

SIZE AND DESCRIPTION Length 33–36mm; hindwing 19–24mm. Red abdomen with black markings. Three female forms, varying in the amount of black on the abdomen.

HABITAT AND DISTRIBUTION Clear streams, ponds, lakes, ditches and canals across Europe except northern Scandinavia, Iceland and Sardinia. Widespread and common in Britain, although it has declined in the last 30 years in areas with intensive cultivation, particularly in eastern England.

FOOD AND HABITS Flies late April–late September, usually in large numbers. Rests on marginal plants. Feeds on small insects.

Blue-tailed Damselfly
Ischnura elegans

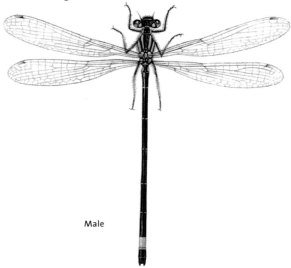

Male

SIZE AND DESCRIPTION Length 30–34mm; hindwing 14–21mm. Metallic
dark bronze/black abdomen with a light-blue band on segment eight.
HABITAT AND DISTRIBUTION Lowland pools and slow-flowing rivers. Usually
the first damselfly to visit newly dug garden ponds. Absent from
Iceland, as well as from much of Spain and Scandinavia.
FOOD AND HABITS Flies early May–early September. Plucks small insects
from waterside vegetation, or captures them from the air. Steady flier.

Northern Damselfly
Coenagrion hastulatum

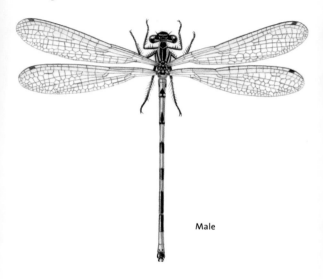

Male

SIZE AND DESCRIPTION Length 31–33mm; hindwing 17–22mm. Male is blue and black. Female is clear green from the side and mostly black from above. Undersides of the eyes and face are bright green in both sexes.
HABITAT AND DISTRIBUTION Mainly a northern European species, and in Britain restricted to sedge-fringed lochans in the Scottish Highlands.
FOOD AND HABITS Flies June–August. Feeds on insects. Flight is slow and weak, and about 20–60cm above water.

Emerald Damselfly
Lestes sponsa

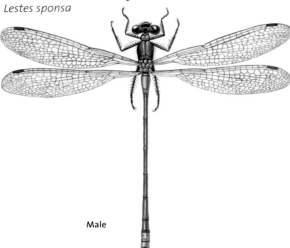

Male

SIZE AND DESCRIPTION Length 26–33mm; hindwing 19–23mm. Male is
metallic green. Mature male is powder blue on the prothorax and
segments 1–2 and 9–10 of the abdomen, and has blue eyes. Female
is duller green, turning to pale brown on the sides of the thorax
and abdomen.

HABITAT AND DISTRIBUTION Ponds, pools, ditches, canals and moorland,
preferably with luxuriant emergent vegetation. Found across central
Europe; locally common throughout Britain in suitable habitats.

FOOD AND HABITS Flies July–September. Feeds mainly on aquatic insects
such as water bugs, mosquitoes and flies. Often perches with its
wings half-open in dense emergent vegetation by shallow ponds.

Red-eyed Damselfly
Erythromma najas

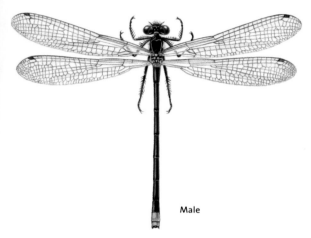

Male

SIZE AND DESCRIPTION Length 33–37mm; hindwing 19–24mm.
Predominantly black with iridescent blue markings. Male is readily
identified by his large, spaced deep red eyes; female has dull red eyes.
HABITAT AND DISTRIBUTION Still water with large expanses of floating
vegetation, including ponds, lakes and canals. Central distribution in
Europe; absent from the far north and Mediterranean. In Britain
found in the south, where it is locally common.
FOOD AND HABITS Flies May–September. Feeds on insects. Males typically
spend much of their time perched on the leaves of floating
vegetation such as water-lilies and algae mats. Strong, direct flight
over water.

Variable Damselfly
Coenagrion pulchellum

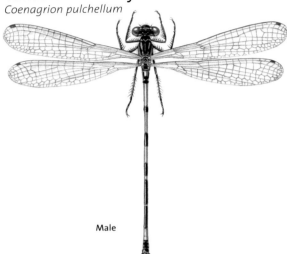

Male

SIZE AND DESCRIPTION Length 23–30mm; hindwing 16–23mm. Can resemble Common Blue and Azure Damselflies, but is more slender, and darker due to the extensive black markings on the thorax and abdomen. Two colour forms, blue and dark, in the female.

HABITAT AND DISTRIBUTION Near-stagnant or slow-flowing water in ponds, ditches, canals and lakes with fringing vegetation. Occurs mainly in central Europe. Found in many parts of Britain, where colonies are often restricted to small areas; common and widespread in Ireland.

FOOD AND HABITS Flies May–August. Feeds on insects. Immature individuals mature away from water, in adjacent meadows, near hedgerows and in tall herbaceous vegetation.

Banded Demoiselle
Calopteryx splendens

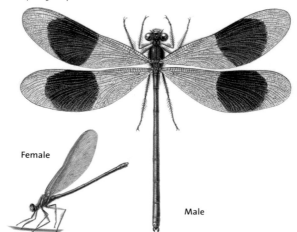

Female

Male

SIZE AND DESCRIPTION Length 45–48mm; hindwing 27–36mm. Wings of male each have a dark blue-black band across the centre. Female's wings are iridescent pale green. Body is metallic blue-green in male, green with a bronze tip in female.

HABITAT AND DISTRIBUTION Slow-flowing lowland streams and rivers, particularly those with muddy bottoms. Occurs in most of Europe. In England restricted to south of Blackpool and Middlesborough, with isolated populations in the Lake District. Occurs in most of Ireland.

FOOD AND HABITS Flies early May–end August. Feeds on insects. Fluttering, butterfly-like flight. Male often performs a fluttering display flight in front of females.

Beautiful Demoiselle
Calopteryx virgo

SIZE AND DESCRIPTION Length 45–49mm; hindwing 24–36mm. With Banded Demoiselle (page 77), the only damselfly species in Britain with obviously coloured wings. Male's wings range from purplish-brown to deep blue-violet, with an iridescent sheen that makes them look brighter in sunlight; those of female are iridescent brown-green. Body colour is metallic blue-green in male, and green with a bronze tip in female. Banded Demoiselle female is similar, but tends to have narrower wings with a brownish tint.

HABITAT AND DISTRIBUTION Fast-flowing streams, particularly those with

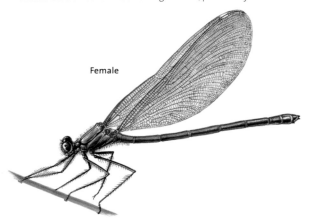

Female

sand or gravel bottoms, often in heathland or moorland areas. Occasionally found in ponds. Widespread and common in many parts of Europe, but not found in the far north. Both Beautiful and Banded Demoiselles are sensitive to pollution.

FOOD AND HABITS Flies late May–end August. Feeds on insects. Fluttering, butterfly-like flight. Larvae live among roots or submerged vegetation, overwintering buried in gravel and emerging with rising temperatures in spring.

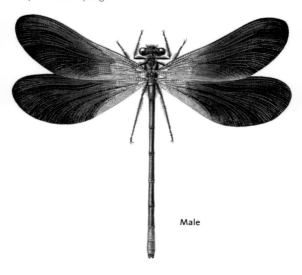

Male

Emperor Dragonfly
Anax imperator

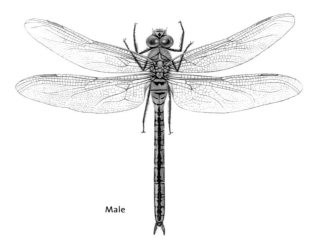

Male

SIZE AND DESCRIPTION Length 66–84mm; hindwing 45–52mm. Male has greenish-blue eyes, an apple-green thorax and a bright blue abdomen with a thick black stripe down the back. Female is usually green, but may be blue.

HABITAT AND DISTRIBUTION Well-vegetated pools, ponds, ditches and slow-flowing rivers across Europe, southwards from Denmark. Visits woodland rides and glades when hunting.

FOOD AND HABITS Flies late May–mid-August. Hunts flies, moths and beetles, and even takes tadpoles from the water's surface. Males fly strongly, patrolling territory above human head height.

Golden-ringed Dragonfly
Cordulegaster boltonii

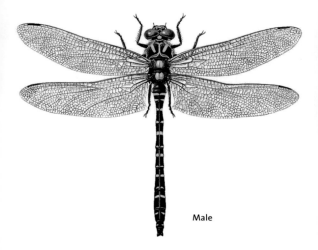

Male

SIZE AND DESCRIPTION Length 74–80mm (m), 80–85mm (f); hindwing 45–51mm. Striking black insect with yellow rings along the abdomen. Female is more parallel-sided than male and has an extremely long ovipositor. Bright green eyes meet at a point on top of the head. One of the largest dragonflies in Britain.

HABITAT AND DISTRIBUTION Acidic rivers and streams; also heathland. Found across Europe except the far north. In Britain common on rivers in southern England, Wales, the Lake District and western Scotland.

FOOD AND HABITS Flies May–September. Feeds on insects. Breeds in relatively fast-flowing streams; female lays eggs in silt.

Southern Hawker
Aeshna cyanea

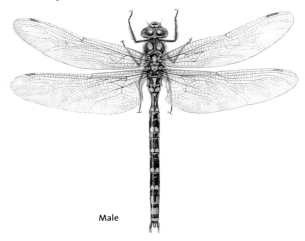

Male

Size and description Length 67–76mm; hindwing 43–53mm. Male is dark with pairs of greenish markings on the first seven abdominal segments, and blue markings on segments 8–10. Female has green markings on her brown abdomen.
Habitat and distribution Ponds, pools and lakes at up to 1,400m, and slow-flowing rivers. Widespread across Europe except the far north.
Food and habits Flies mid-June–October. Adults feed on flying insects. Nymphs eat aquatic insects, tadpoles and small fish. Males fly at human waist height and are inquisitive.

Azure Hawker
Aeshna caerulea

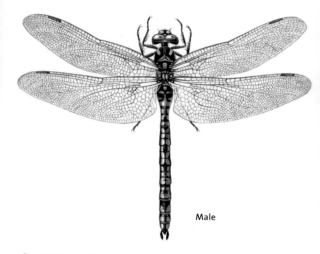

Male

SIZE AND DESCRIPTION Length 57–67mm; hindwing 38–41mm. Mature male is more blue than other hawkers. Female is yellowish or blue.

HABITAT AND DISTRIBUTION Bog pools in moorland. Found in northern Scandinavia and central Europe's higher mountains. In Britain occurs only in Scotland.

FOOD AND HABITS Flies late May–June. Feeds on insects. Basks on stones and tree trunks, and flies low and fast in sunshine, investigating the edges of bog pools. Shelters in heather or similar low vegetation in dull weather.

Brown Hawker
Aeshna grandis

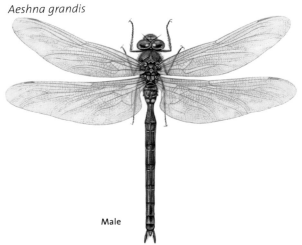

Male

SIZE AND DESCRIPTION Length 70–77mm; hindwing 41–49mm.
Unmistakable brown wings. Male has a brown abdomen with bright
blue spots. Female has yellow markings on her brown abdomen. Both
sexes have diagonal marks on the sides of the thorax.

HABITAT AND DISTRIBUTION Woodland ponds, lakes, canals, peat bogs and
slow-flowing rivers. Occurs in much of Europe except the far north
and south. Very common in lowland Wales and England, more local
further north and with isolated populations in Scotland.

FOOD AND HABITS Flies mid-June–mid-October. Hunts flies, mosquitoes,
moths and butterflies. Strong flier. Males characteristically hover low
down near human observers.

Migrant Hawker
Aeshna mixta

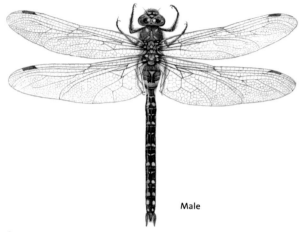

Male

SIZE AND DESCRIPTION Length 56–64mm; hindwing 37–42mm. Dark brown and blue male has a bright blue spot on the side at the base of the abdomen. Brown female has small yellow spots.

HABITAT AND DISTRIBUTION Still or slow-flowing water including ponds, gravel pits, lakes, canals and slow-running rivers. Distributed from England and Wales across Europe, south from the Baltic to North Africa. Until the 1940s, an uncommon migrant from southern Europe, but has gradually increased its range from a breeding population in south-east England, where it is now common. Migrations from the Continent increase British population in late summer.

FOOD AND HABITS Flies July–October. Feeds on insects. Approachable. Neat, elegant and sometimes jerky flight.

Common Hawker
Aeshna juncea

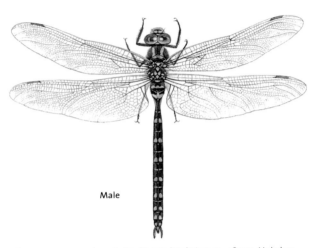

Male

SIZE AND DESCRIPTION Length 65–80mm; hindwing 40–48mm. Male has a black abdomen with blue spots and small yellow marks. Female is brown with yellow marks.

HABITAT AND DISTRIBUTION A variety of still waters, including ponds, lakes, peat bogs and still pools. Found south from northern Norway to the Pyrenees; absent from Iceland.

FOOD AND HABITS Flies late June–October. Hawks for other insects, often some way from water. Flies well and strongly – males spend long periods on the wing and rarely perch.

Northern Emerald
Somatochlora arctica

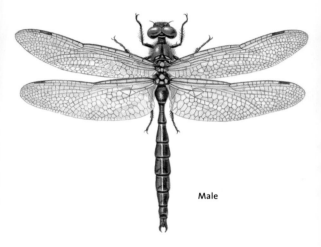

Male

SIZE AND DESCRIPTION Length 40–55mm; hindwing 34–36mm. Very dark green-black, with orange-yellow markings on the sides of segments 2–3, which are larger in female than in male. Male has a characteristic, obviously waisted abdomen.

HABITAT AND DISTRIBUTION Peat-bog pools. Found mainly in northern and central Europe, including Scotland and south-west Ireland.

FOOD AND HABITS Flies late May–end September. Feeds on insects. Patrols pools at about a metre above the water, and flies fast and straight at tree-top height when feeding.

Brilliant Emerald
Somatochlora metallica

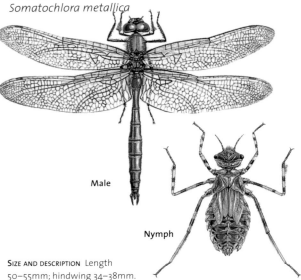

Male

Nymph

SIZE AND DESCRIPTION Length
50–55mm; hindwing 34–38mm.
Dark metallic emerald-green body with a bright bronze sheen. Eyes
are apple-green. Wings are suffused with saffron, particularly in
female. Male has a slightly club-shaped abdomen.

HABITAT AND DISTRIBUTION Lowland marshes, fens and wet meadows,
mainly in central and northern Europe. Scarce in Britain, but locally
common where it occurs in the Scottish Highlands and south-east
England. Threatened by inappropriate management, deforestation,
water-level reduction, pollution and the introduction of fish.

FOOD AND HABITS Flies June–mid-August. Feeds on insects.

Downy Emerald
Cordulia aenea

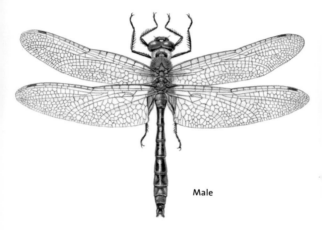

Male

Size and description Length 50mm; hindwing 29–35mm. Dark, metallic greenish-bronze abdomen, slightly club-shaped in male, and bright apple-green eyes; immature individuals have brown eyes. Thorax is coated with fine hairs. One of the three emeralds found in Britain.
Habitat and distribution Sheltered woodland ponds, lakes and canals with some overhanging shrubs and trees. Occurs in northern and central regions on the Continent, and locally in southern Britain, the Scottish Highlands, southern Ireland and a few other places.
Food and habits Flies mid-May–mid-July. Feeds on insects. Low and fast flight, rarely more than a metre above water, interspersed with periods of hovering.

Four-spotted Chaser
Libellula quadrimaculata

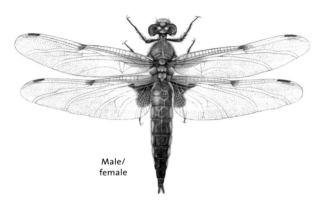

Male/
female

SIZE AND DESCRIPTION Length 40–48mm; hindwing 32–40mm. Broad brown body with yellow patches along each side and black at the tip. Two dark marks on the leading edge of each wing.

HABITAT AND DISTRIBUTION Still water with plenty of vegetation. Found throughout Europe except Iceland. Widespread in Britain, but not found in many parts of north-east England.

FOOD AND HABITS Flies mid-May–mid-August. Feeds on insects. Frequently perches in the open and flies out over the water. Aggressive and territorial nature.

Broad-bodied Chaser
Libellula depressa

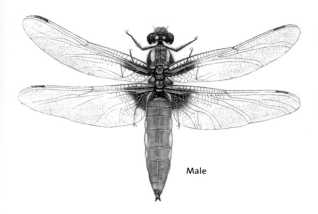

Male

SIZE AND DESCRIPTION Length 39–48mm; hindwing 32–38mm. Male has a flattened, fat pale blue body with yellow patches along each side. Brownish-yellow female and immatures have yellow spots along each side, and look rather like giant wasps.

HABITAT AND DISTRIBUTION Still or slow-flowing water at up to 1,200m. Distributed across Europe from Wales and England, and from southern Sweden south to the Mediterranean.

FOOD AND HABITS Flies early May–early August. Feeds on insects. Tends to rest on waterside plants. Fast flier.

Scarce Chaser
Libellula fulva

SIZE AND DESCRIPTION Length 41–48mm; hindwing 35–38mm. Mature male has a powder-blue abdomen with the last three segments black, and blue-grey eyes. Immature males and females are vivid orange with dark bases to the wings.

HABITAT AND DISTRIBUTION River floodplains and water meadows, and sometimes gravel pits and nearby ponds, favouring areas with prolific emergent vegetation and bushes. Found in mainland Europe north to southern Fenno-Scandinavia. Scarce in Britain, occurring only in southern England.

FOOD AND HABITS Flies end May–early August. Feeds on insects. Basks on the top of dense vegetation. Flight is darting, often pausing to hover.

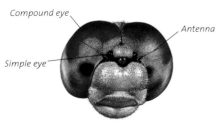

Compound eye

Antenna

Simple eye

Head of a Dragonfly
Dragonflies and damselflies have the biggest eyes of any insect, with superb all-round colour vision for seeing other insects in flight. The eyes are compound, made up of around 30,000 facets (ommatidia). Dragonflies' eyes are much closer together than damselflies' eyes, which are at the outer ends of the head. There are also three simple eyes (ocelli), each made up of a single lens, which inform the insect of its attitude when in flight. Spending most of their time flying and rarely in contact with a hard surface, these insects do not need feelers. Their antennae are thus relatively smaller than those of most other insects.

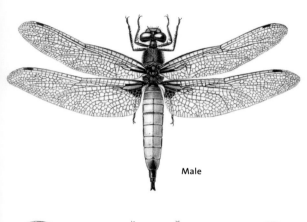

Male

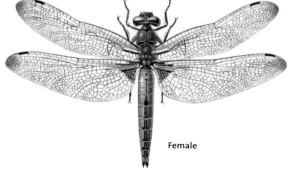

Female

Black-tailed Skimmer
Orthetrum cancellatum

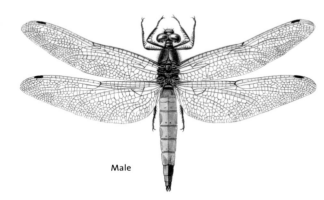

Male

SIZE AND DESCRIPTION Length 45–50mm; hindwing 35–38mm. In mature male, segments 1–2 are brown, 3–7 blue and 8–10 black, with yellow spots laterally; eyes are blue. Female is yellow with two rows of black streaks down the abdomen, and brown eyes.

HABITAT AND DISTRIBUTION Ponds and lakes mainly in lowland areas, where bankside vegetation is not too dense. Found in most of Europe except Scotland and the far north.

FOOD AND HABITS Flies May–August. Favours relatively large prey such as butterflies, damselflies and grasshoppers. Highly active and fast flying; often skims the water's surface near to shore, and males see off other males from favoured perches such as rocks, stones, logs and bare ground. They are very aggressive – a male may have a territory of more than 50m of a bank.

Keeled Skimmer
Orthetrum coerulescens

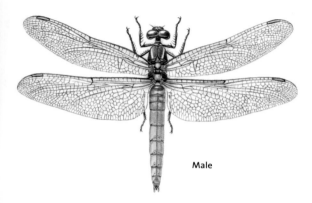

Male

SIZE AND DESCRIPTION Length 40–45mm; hindwing 28–34mm. Male has a blue body and eyes. Female is light brown, with age darkening to nearly black, with a black line down the centre of the upper surface, and brown or grey eyes.

HABITAT AND DISTRIBUTION Small rivers, runnels, streams, ditches and swampy pools in acid-peat regions, typically with sphagnum moss. Occurs in western and central Europe. Patchily distributed and locally common in Britain, mainly in the west and Ireland.

FOOD AND HABITS Flies June–August. Feeds on insects. Males have small territories that they observe from the ground or low perches. Wings are held well forwards when at rest. Fast and erratic flight with brief spells of hovering.

Black Darter
Sympetrum danae

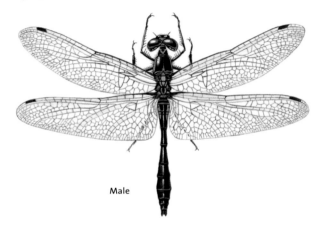

Male

SIZE AND DESCRIPTION Length 30–35mm; hindwing 20–30mm. Mature male is largely black on the upper surface, and has a waisted abdomen. Female and immature males have a yellow abdomen with extensive black markings.

HABITAT AND DISTRIBUTION Mainly shallow acidic-peaty pools with abundant emergent vegetation. Northern species found in Europe and Canada. Widespread and can be abundant in Britain, particularly in the north.

FOOD AND HABITS Flies June–September. Feeds on insects. Erratic and short flight, often perching in vegetation near pools.

White-faced Darter
Leucorrhinia dubia

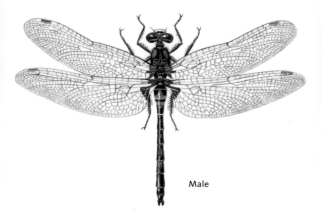

Male

SIZE AND DESCRIPTION Length 21–27mm; hindwing 23–28mm. Mature male has a narrow black abdomen with red or orange on the front and rear segments, which can darken with age; in flight can appear almost black. Female and immature males are mainly black, with pale yellow front and rear markings.

HABITAT AND DISTRIBUTION Acidic bog pools with rafts of sphagnum moss for egg laying, in lowland peat bogs. Found throughout northern Europe east to Siberia. In Britain it is a mainly northern species, and has declined, notably in England, due to habitat destruction.

FOOD AND HABITS Flies late May–early August. Feeds on insects. Flies in a skittish manner, frequently hovering low over water, and settling on bare peaty soil patches and low vegetation near pool margins.

Common Darter
Sympetrum striolatum

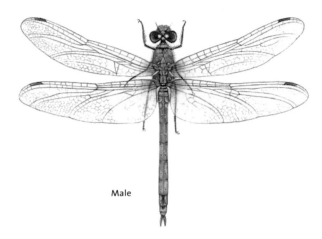

Male

SIZE AND DESCRIPTION Length 35–44mm; hindwing 24–30mm. Mature male is red with a narrow pointed abdomen. Female and immatures are yellowish to light brown.

HABITAT AND DISTRIBUTION Ponds, lakes, ditches and brackish waters at up to 1,800m. Distributed across Europe from Ireland, and south from southern Scandinavia to North Africa.

FOOD AND HABITS Flies June–October. Feeds on insects. Usually seen in large numbers. Flies busily. Often perches on twigs.

Ruddy Darter
Sympetrum sanguineum

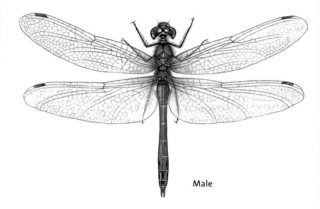

Male

SIZE AND DESCRIPTION Length 34–39mm; hindwing 23–31mm. Male is blood-red with a club-shaped rather than tapering abdomen. Yellow female has black thorax markings.

HABITAT AND DISTRIBUTION Shallow and well-vegetated (even brackish or acid) ponds, pools, lakes, ditches and canals at up to 1,000m. Occurs from Ireland across Europe, and south from southern Scandinavia. British population, which is strongest in south-east England, is supplemented by immigrants from the Continent in summer.

FOOD AND HABITS Flies June–October. Feeds on insects. Flitting and sometimes jerky flight. Often perches.

Water cricket
Velia caprai

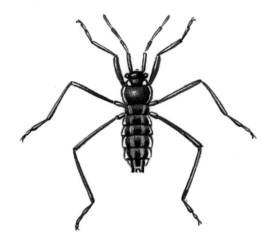

SIZE AND DESCRIPTION Length to 8mm. Mainly brown with orange along the back. Stouter body than those of either pond skaters or Common Water Measurer (opposite).

HABITAT AND DISTRIBUTION Widespread and common on still and slow-moving water in ponds, lakes and rivers in Britain and other parts of Europe.

FOOD AND HABITS Tiny predator that lives on the water's surface. Locates prey by sight, detecting ripples on the water's surface. It is distasteful to predatory fish.

Common Water Measurer
Hydrometra stagnorum

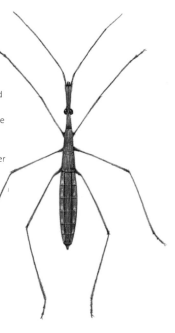

SIZE AND DESCRIPTION Length to
12mm. Narrow body, greatly
elongated head and long
legs. Usually wingless.
Lesser Water Measurer
(*H. gracilenta*), the only other
water measurer species found
in Britain, is much rarer.
HABITAT AND DISTRIBUTION Surface
of still or slow-flowing water
throughout much of Europe.
FOOD AND HABITS Feeds on water
fleas, insect larvae and other
small animals, which it
spears from the surface
with its beak. Sensitive
to vibrations in the
surface film of the
water, using them
to locate prey. Also
hunts by sitting on the
surface and catching
water fleas and other
small animals moving
underneath. Moves slowly
across the water's surface.

Common Pond Skater
Gerris lacustris

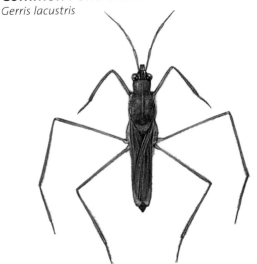

Size and description Length to 10mm. Broader body than that of
Common Water Measurer (page 101) and a considerably shorter head,
which has largish eyes. Usually fully winged. Several similar species.
Habitat and distribution Ponds, lakes and slow-running rivers
throughout Europe.
Food and habits Senses vibrations made by other insects. 'Skates' over
the surface of the water, moving with a rowing action of the middle
legs. The hindlegs act as rudders, while the front legs catch insects
that fall into the water. Flies away from water in order to hibernate.

Water Scorpion
Nepa cinerea

SIZE AND DESCRIPTION Length to 22mm; tail to 8mm. Flattened brown body equipped with strong, scorpion-like front legs and a snorkel at the rear. Fully winged, but rarely flies.

HABITAT AND DISTRIBUTION Shallow still water and pond margins. Occurs across Europe.

FOOD AND HABITS Walks slowly over plants or mud just under the water. Breathes through its hollow, snorkel-like 'tail', which draws in air as it protrudes above the surface. Active throughout the year, feeding on invertebrates and small fish, which are caught with its powerful front legs.

Water Stick Insect
Ranatra linearis

Size and description Length to 50mm. Huge pincers and a long air tube at the hind end like that of Water Scorpion (page 103), to which it is closely related.

Habitat and distribution Weedy still-water ponds and lakes. Widely distributed throughout Europe except the far north and south. Fairly common in southern England and Wales.

Food and habits Adopts a mantid-like posture when submerged and ambushes passing aquatic creatures, catching them with its front legs. Looks rather like a twig, and this camouflage helps it to creep up on its prey. The breathing tube is stuck out through the surface of the water to breathe air.

Common Backswimmer
Notonecta glauca

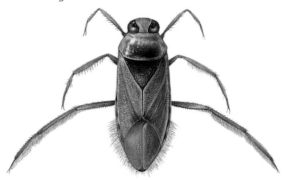

Swimming position

SIZE AND DESCRIPTION Length to 17mm. Long and bristly hindlegs. One of several species of water boatman. Also called Great Water Boatman, but true water boatmen (page 106) swim with the dorsal surface uppermost.

HABITAT AND DISTRIBUTION Common in ponds, lakes and slow-running rivers across Britain and continental Europe.

FOOD AND HABITS A fierce hunter of tadpoles, small fish and other insects. Swims on its back, which is keeled, clutching a large air-bubble to its underside and 'rowing' with its back legs. Active all year round. Will fly in warm weather.

Punctate Corixa
Corixa punctata

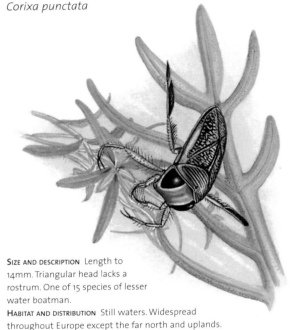

SIZE AND DESCRIPTION Length to
14mm. Triangular head lacks a
rostrum. One of 15 species of lesser
water boatman.

HABITAT AND DISTRIBUTION Still waters. Widespread
throughout Europe except the far north and uplands.

FOOD AND HABITS Feeds on plant debris and microscopic organisms.
Swims with its back upwards, unlike the similar-looking Common
Backswimmer (page 105). Courting male sings loudly by rubbing
the hair patches on the insides of his front legs against his head.
Capable of flight.

Alder-fly
Sialis lutaria

SIZE AND DESCRIPTION Length to 15mm. Robust brown body with two pairs of glossy brown or grey, dark-veined wings that are folded back over the body, tent-like, when at rest.

HABITAT AND DISTRIBUTION Common near lakes and rivers.

FOOD AND HABITS Adults are found near water in April–October, sometimes in vast numbers, and live for only a few days to breed. Eggs are laid on vegetation, and larvae descend into the water after hatching, where they prey on other invertebrates. They turn into adults after 1–2 years.

Aquatic Insect Larvae

Many insects lay their eggs in water, and their larvae live underwater until the adult insects are ready to emerge. They include mosquitoes, beetles (page 121), midges, and some crane-flies and hover-flies, as well as the distinctive groups described on these pages.

Dragonfly Nymphs

Nymphs of dragonflies are voracious feeders that live underwater. Easy to distinguish from damselfly nymphs, they are shorter, stouter, often much fatter and have gills in a hollow in the abdomen. They do not swim, but can propel themselves over short distances by expelling air. Nymphs of the big hawkers, mainly of the *Aeshna* genus, are to 50mm long and can catch animals as big as tadpoles and small fish. They spend 1–3 years in the larval stage before emerging as dragonflies.

Damselfly Nymphs

Like dragonfly nymphs, damselfly nymphs are fierce carnivores that may exist for several years at the larval stage. They are slender, with a tapering abdomen ending in three feathery 'tails', which are gills. The legs are long and slender, and they are usually green, olive or pale brown. They swim with undulations of the body.

Mayfly Larvae

These larvae are relatively common, and similar to damselfly nymphs. They measure to about 20mm in length, and have gills along the sides of the body that may be feathery and obvious, or inconspicuous. They metamorphose into mayflies en masse in late spring.

Caddis Fly Larvae

The larvae of caddis flies use underwater debris to form protective camouflaged cases to  50mm long around themselves. As soon as it emerges from an egg, a larva begins winding a sticky thread around itself, attaching particles from its environment until it is covered. Stones, sand, twigs and plant stems are utilized, and a larva lives in the case for up to a year. The pupa then cuts itself free, wriggles to the surface and splits, and the adult fly emerges. Each of nearly 200 British caddis fly species can be identified by its case construction.

Alder-fly Larvae

The larvae of alder-flies have large heads with powerful jaws used for feeding on smaller insects. They have three pairs of legs and a pair of limb-like, feathery gills on each body segment except the last one, which is tipped with a long, spike-like gill. Tail tapers to a single point.

Caddis fly
Phryganea grandis

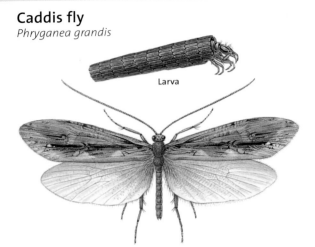

Larva

SIZE AND DESCRIPTION Length 20–30mm; wingspan 64mm. Largest
caddis fly in Britain. Resembles a small moth with short hairs on the
wings. Long antennae are almost the length of the broad dusty-
brown wings. Male is smaller than female and lacks the black stripe in
her forewing. Holds wings over the body like a tent when at rest.
HABITAT AND DISTRIBUTION Slow-moving rivers and streams across most
of Europe, but not the far south.
FOOD AND HABITS Flies May–November. Feeds on plants and other insect
larvae. Flies mostly at night and is attracted to light. In the species
described here, the larva's case is made from spirally arranged cut
sections of aquatic leaves, each piece butted to the next. Adults live
for about a week.

Bicoloured Sedge
Triaenodes bicolor

Larva

SIZE AND DESCRIPTION
Wingspan 16–20mm.
Rich chestnut-brown
caddis fly with dark grey
hindwings. Antennae are
cream with black rings, and
may be three times as long
as the body length.
HABITAT AND DISTRIBUTION
Ponds and lakes. Found in
Europe east to western Russia.
FOOD AND HABITS Flies June–
September. Active during the
day. Adults feed only on liquids
such as nectar and sap; larvae
feed on green plants. Female
deposits eggs in a spiral pattern on
aquatic plants. Ochre-yellow larvae
construct slender straight cases of spirally
arranged root sections or narrow leaf.

Brown China-mark
Elophila nymphaeata

SIZE AND DESCRIPTION Wingspan 22–30mm. Variable species, with some individuals being quite dark and dull looking, others with delicate patterns of white patches and streaks.

HABITAT AND DISTRIBUTION Common in stagnant or slow-flowing water around ponds, lakes and canals throughout Britain.

FOOD AND HABITS Flies June–August. Larva makes a flat oval case from floating pondweed or water-lily leaf pieces. Cocoon is covered with leaf pieces and attached to a stem or leaf below and above the water's surface.

Beautiful China-mark
Nymphula stagnata

SIZE AND DESCRIPTION Wingspan 18–25mm. Pale wings with distinctive dark brown markings. China-mark moths are unique among British Lepidoptera in passing their immature stages underwater. Five native species in Britain.

HABITAT AND DISTRIBUTION Common and widely distributed around ponds, lakes and rivers throughout Britain.

FOOD AND HABITS Flies July–August in the evening and at night. Eggs are laid on the undersides of leaves of floating plants such as burr-reed. Initially living in the tissues of the plant, a larva later makes a protective case from leaf pieces. It pupates in a white cocoon attached to a leaf, partially or wholly submerged.

Ringed China-mark
Parapoynx stratiotata

SIZE AND DESCRIPTION Wingspan 15–28mm. Female is larger than male. Colour is variable, but there is always a dark ring with a whitish centre on the forewing.

HABITAT AND DISTRIBUTION Widely distributed and relatively common in southern Britain.

FOOD AND HABITS Flies June–August. Larva joins together water plant leaves and stems, creating a more open shelter than Brown China-mark (page 112). Cocoon is large and oval and always fastened to a submerged stem.

Small China-mark
Cataclysta lemnata

SIZE AND DESCRIPTION Wingspan 18–24mm. Male is smaller and paler than female, but both sexes have a characteristic row of blue-centred black dots on the outer fringe of the hindwing.

HABITAT AND DISTRIBUTION Common near ponds and other small waterbodies with ample surface duckweed throughout Britain.

FOOD AND HABITS Flies June–August. Dark grey larva is aquatic, feeding only on floating duckweed and sheltering just under the water's surface in a little tubular case made from pieces of the food plant. It pupates in a silken cocoon inside the air bubble in the case.

Large Crane-fly
Tipula maxima

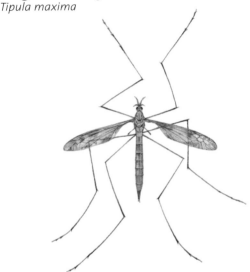

SIZE AND DESCRIPTION Length almost 30mm; wingspan 65mm.
Distinctive mottled brown wings, which are held at right angles when
at rest. Female has a pointed abdomen, male a blunted abdomen. The
largest of 300 British crane-fly species, with a leg span of 100mm.
HABITAT AND DISTRIBUTION Wooded areas in much of Europe.
FOOD AND HABITS Adults fly April–August. Female lays eggs in the damp
mossy fringes of ponds, streams and ditches. Larvae are aquatic, living
just below the water's surface, then continuing to develop in
submerged leaf litter.

Chironomid Midge
Chironomus plumosus

Length 8mm. Wings are shorter than the abdomen and held over the body at rest. Male's antennae are very bushy. Reddish aquatic larva is known as a 'bloodworm'. Must have a body of water in which to lay eggs. This may be relatively small, for example a water butt. Adults rest on walls as they dry out after emerging from the pupae. Non-biting.

Common Gnat
Culex pipiens

Length 6mm. Wings extend beyond the abdomen's tip. Female has a rounded tip to her abdomen. Male has hairy antennae. Holds abdomen parallel to the surface on which it is perching. Abundant in Europe. Flies at night with a monotonous hum. Rarely bites humans, preferring birds. Aquatic larvae live under the water's surface. Eggs are laid in rafts on the water's surface, and the larvae dangle beneath it. Pupae swim to the bottom to escape danger. Adults may hibernate over winter.

Mosquito
Theobaldia annulata

Length 6mm. The largest mosquito. White rings around the legs, and dark spots on the wings formed by convergences of veins. Widespread where there is stagnant water for breeding, including around ponds. Adult females are blood sucking and require blood in order to lay fertile eggs. Males feed on nectar and the juices of plants. Females hibernate in sheds.

Clegg-fly
Haematopota pluvialis

Length 11mm. Dull grey horsefly with a rather cylindrical abdomen. Wings are mottled, and held above the abdomen when at rest. Flies silently. Common in May–September, especially in damp woods. Replaced in northern and upland areas by a similar species. Flies May–October. Most active in humid and overcast weather. Females are bloodsuckers, biting both humans and livestock. Males drink nectar and plant juices. Larvae live in damp soil, where they prey on other invertebrates.

Whirligig beetle
Gyrinus natator

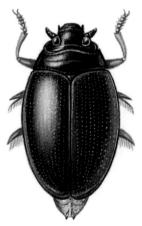

SIZE AND DESCRIPTION Length 6–7mm. Tiny shiny black beetle that gyrates on the water's surface and dives rapidly when alarmed. Middle and hind legs are short and oar-like. Two-part eyes enable it to look down into the water and across the surface simultaneously. The most common of 12 whirligig beetle species in Britain.
HABITAT AND DISTRIBUTION Still and slow-moving water across Europe.
FOOD AND HABITS Visible for much of the year, though it hibernates. Preys on mosquito larvae and insects that fall into the water. Dives rapidly down into the water when disturbed. Often seen in small groups. Lays eggs on submerged plants. Larvae stay on the bottom until they are nearly fully grown.

Lesser Diving Beetle
Colymbetes fuscus

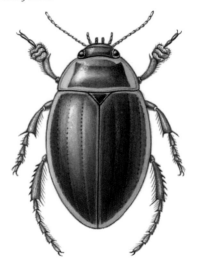

SIZE AND DESCRIPTION Length 17–19mm. Rather like a small Great Diving Beetle (opposite), but smoother and more uniformly oval in shape. Often has a green iridescence.

HABITAT AND DISTRIBUTION Stagnant weedy ponds and ditches throughout central and northern Europe.

FOOD AND HABITS Can be found during most of the year, although it may hibernate during the coldest winter months. A predator of other invertebrates.

Great Diving Beetle
Dytiscus marginalis

SIZE AND DESCRIPTION Length
27–35mm. Olive-green to black,
fringed with yellowish-brown.
Females have ridged elytra (wing
cases in beetles), while males have
smooth ones. Larva is 60mm long
and has well-developed legs
and a segmented body that
bends more than that of a
dragonfly nymph (page 108).
HABITAT AND DISTRIBUTION
Reedy ponds and other
still waters. The most
common European
diving beetle.
FOOD AND HABITS Flies at night.
Prey includes newts, tadpoles,
small fish and insects. Larvae
live underwater and are
voracious predators.

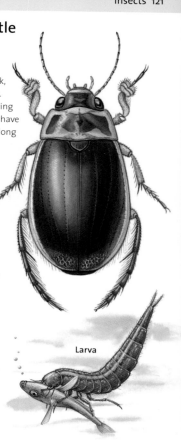

Larva

Diving beetle
Hydroporus palustris

SIZE AND DESCRIPTION Length 3–3.3mm. Oval-shaped elytra. Black with patches of reddish or yellowish-brown. One of 34 species in a genus of diving water beetles found in Europe.

HABITAT AND DISTRIBUTION Common in all types of still water throughout central and northern Europe.

FOOD AND HABITS Flies at night. Preys on a variety of small aquatic invertebrates. Comes to the surface for air, which it carries in a bubble beneath its elytra when it dives.

Water scavenger beetle
Hydrobins fuscipes

Size and description Length 6–9mm. Black with a metallic sheen. Can be distinguished by the pitted furrows along the elytra. Legs are rust in colour. Very flat underside. Larva is maggot-like.

Habitat and distribution Still waters throughout Europe.

Food and habits Omnivorous scavenger that does not swim well and crawls over underwater plants. Collects air from the surface by swimming to it head first and storing it beneath its elytra. Larvae are predatory on other aquatic invertebrates.

Screech-beetle
Hygrobia hermanni

SIZE AND DESCRIPTION Length to 8–12mm. Convex, dull rusty-brown beetle with a black edge around the thorax and prominent eyes. Name derives from the sound it makes when it is picked up, by rubbing the tip of its abdomen against its elytra.

HABITAT AND DISTRIBUTION Muddy-bottomed still-water bodies such as ponds and ditches. Widespread in Europe, except the far north and Mediterranean. In Britain has a mainly central–southerly distribution.

FOOD AND HABITS Feeds on worms. Larva is about 12mm long. It pupates out of the water, the life cycle taking less than four months.

Great Silver Beetle
Hydrophilus piceus

SIZE AND DESCRIPTION
Length 40–50mm.
Shiny and black
scavenger
beetle with
a high-domed back,
greenish sheen, reddish
antennae and velvet-like
hairs underneath that
trap air bubbles. One of
the largest insects in Britain.

HABITAT AND DISTRIBUTION Very weedy, mud-bottomed pools and fens.
Once common in Britain, but becoming scarce and endangered, and
absent from northern Britain.

FOOD AND HABITS Capable of flight, which takes place at night.
Hibernates during winter in mud at the bottoms of ponds. Larvae are
to 75mm long, and found in weedy ponds, especially those covered in
duckweed. They are carnivorous, consuming snails and tadpoles, and
pupate in damp earth at the sides of ponds.

Red Water Mite
Hydrachna globulosus

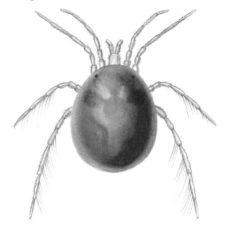

SIZE AND DESCRIPTION Length to 2mm. Rich deep red. Looks like a small spider, but its rounded body is not divided into two parts; like a spider, it has eight legs. One of about 300 species in Britain, which are difficult to distinguish from each other. They are abundant, and often brilliantly coloured and patterned; the brighter species may easily be seen on the surface of the water.

HABITAT AND DISTRIBUTION Widespread in ponds and lake margins.

FOOD AND HABITS Water mites are predators, feeding on small invertebrates like water fleas, water lice and blood worms. The fluid content of prey is sucked out via piercing mouthparts. The larvae of some species are parasitic on aquatic insects such as diving beetles, attaching themselves to a host.

Common Pirate Spider
Pirata piraticus

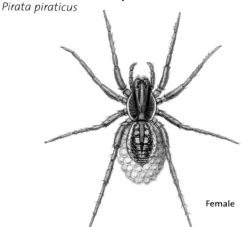

Female

Size and description Length to 9mm (f); to 6mm (m). Semi-aquatic wolf spider. Carapace is dark green-brown with an elongated 'V' mark. Dark abdomen with a velvety iridescence marked with purple and white spots.

Habitat and distribution Edges of ponds, marshes and lakes. Common and widespread in Europe.

Food and habits Unable to live away from water, hunting on the water's surface and on banks; capable of walking on water. Spins a white silken tube in moss and similar vegetation, which opens at or just above the water level. Stays inside the tube with its forelegs protruding and resting on the water. On sensing vibrations on the water's surface, it emerges at great speed to try and catch prey. The upper open end of the tube can be closed by drawing across a silk veil.

Raft Spider
Dolomedes fimbriatus

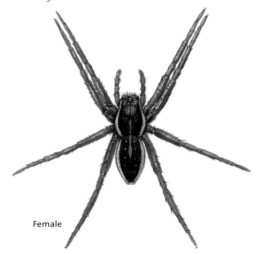

Female

SIZE AND DESCRIPTION Length to 22mm; leg span to 70mm (f). Male is much smaller than female. One of the two largest spiders in Britain. Dark chocolate-brown, sometimes greenish, with a conspicuous white or cream stripe along each side. Also called Fishing Spider and Swamp Spider.

HABITAT AND DISTRIBUTION Lives around ponds, lakes, swamps and slow-flowing streams. Widespread but often local or scarce across Europe.

FOOD AND HABITS Hunts by spreading its legs on the water's surface to detect ripples from insects, and also vibrates its legs in order to attract prey.

Common Stretch-spider
Tetragnatha extensa

SIZE AND DESCRIPTION Length to 11mm (f); to 9mm (m). Elongated cream-coloured body. Four pairs of very long and dark yellow legs. Carapace is orange or dark yellow.

HABITAT AND DISTRIBUTION Low vegetation in damp areas. Wide distribution across the northern hemisphere, and one of the most common spiders in Britain.

FOOD AND HABITS Feeds on flying insects such as mosquitoes, midges and moths, which it catches in its web. Adopts a straight-line posture for camouflage when alarmed, sitting along a plant stem, blade of grass or central leaf vein with its four front legs pointing forwards and back legs pointing backwards. Capable of walking on water, where it moves faster than on land.

Male

Female, camouflage posture

Water Spider
Argyroneta aquatica

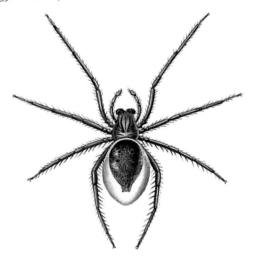

SIZE AND DESCRIPTION Length to 15mm. Brown and rather mouse-like.
HABITAT AND DISTRIBUTION Ponds, lakes, dykes and sluggish streams across Europe.
FOOD AND HABITS Builds a diving bell by trapping air in the middle of a sheet-like web spun among pond plants underwater. Visits the surface and collects air between the hairs on its abdomen, releasing this into the diving bell by stroking the hairs on its back legs. Lives in the bell, leaving it only to hunt for small fish, tadpoles and other pond life. May spend winter sealed inside an old snail's shell.

Three-spined Stickleback
Gastroeseus aculeatus

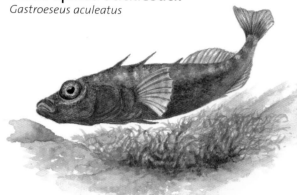

SIZE AND DESCRIPTION Length to 10cm. Dark brown-green above and silver below. Three heavy spines along the back. Male develops a red chin and belly in the breeding season, as shown here. Nine-spined Stickleback (*Pungitius pungitius*) is smaller, has a thinner body and is rarer.

HABITAT AND DISTRIBUTION Weedy ponds, lakes and rivers, as well as estuaries and seashore pools. Widespread and often common. Native to much of northern Europe.

FOOD AND HABITS Diet includes small molluscs, crustaceans and insect larvae. Male builds a nest on the bottom of a water body from vegetation, sand, pebbles and other debris. He performs a zigzag courtship dance in spring to entice a female, then guards and maintains the nest and eggs, fanning the eggs to ensure a fresh water supply and threatening any fish (particularly red ones) that come too near. Lifespan up to three years.

European Perch
Percia fluviatilis

SIZE AND DESCRIPTION Length to 50cm. Female normally grows larger than male. Greenish with red pelvic, anal and caudal fins, and 5–9 vertical dark bars on the sides.

HABITAT AND DISTRIBUTION Ponds, lowland lakes and slow-flowing rivers. Found across Europe, including Britain, and widely introduced elsewhere.

FOOD AND HABITS
Carnivorous, feeding on other fish. Spawns in spring, depositing eggs in lacy bands on water plants, stones, or tree or shrub branches immersed in water. Males may be sexually mature at 6–12 months, and young perch swim in shoals. Older perch tend to be solitary. Lifespan up to 22 years.

Common Eel
Anguilla anguilla

SIZE AND DESCRIPTION Length to 1.5m; usually 60–80cm. Long, narrow and rope-like fish. Adult is dark brown on the back, yellow beneath.
HABITAT AND DISTRIBUTION Ditches, pools, lakes, fens and lowland rivers. Critically Endangered due to factors including overfishing, parasites and man-made barriers to migration.
FOOD AND HABITS Freshwater eels are mainly nocturnal, and their prey includes pond snails, freshwater shrimps, frogs, tadpoles and fish eggs. Able to survive out of water for long periods, and wriggle over land from one water stretch to another. Adult eels in Europe travel to the sea to breed, crossing the Atlantic Ocean to the Sargasso Sea, where they spawn and probably die. The flat transparent larvae make their way to Europe, reaching to 9cm and transforming into eels that are still transparent (glass eels) on the way. They develop into elvers, then the adult form, in fresh water. On their way back to the sea they become silvery (silver eels). Lifespan up to 50 years.

Gudgeon
Gobio gobio

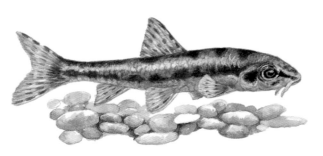

SIZE AND DESCRIPTION Length to 20cm. Light or dark brown back, dorsal fins and tail, marked with characteristic dark spots, and flattened white underside. Barbel on each corner of the mouth.

HABITAT AND DISTRIBUTION Gravel-pit lakes, ponds, canals and rivers across much of Europe.

FOOD AND HABITS Uses barbels to sense food, consisting mainly of invertebrates, on the bottoms of water bodies. Often shoals, remaining on the bottom. Spawning occurs in April–July. Young are mature in 2–3 years and live for 4–6.

Common Carp
Cyprinus carpio

SIZE AND DESCRIPTION Length 60cm or more. Selectively bred for centuries, resulting in a variety of forms. King carp (shown here) is most common in Britain. It is usually greenish-brown above and yellowish below, with uniform scales all over the body. Leather carp lack scales, and mirror carp have a single row of large scales along each side. There is a barbel at each corner of the mouth and two shorter ones on the upper lip.

HABITAT AND DISTRIBUTION Widespread in muddy-bottomed larger ponds and lakes rich in plant life. Originated in Asia, from where it spread naturally to central Europe; introduced to Britain in medieval times.

FOOD AND HABITS Feeds mainly on the bottom on water plants, worms and crustaceans. Spawns in early summer in shallow water at water temperatures of at least 18°C. Lifespan of more than 40 years recorded.

Common Bream
Abramis brama

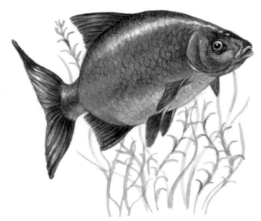

SIZE AND DESCRIPTION Length to 80cm; usually 30–55cm. Very deep and laterally flattened brown body, and small head. Fins are dark at maturity; young bream are silver. Other cyprinids found in ponds include Rudd (*Scardinius erythrophthalmus*) and Roach (*Rutilus rutilus*), both of which have slim silver bodies and reddish fins.
HABITAT AND DISTRIBUTION Slow-moving rivers, canals, ponds, gravel pits and lakes throughout most of Europe.
FOOD AND HABITS Bottom feeder preying on insect larvae, worms and molluscs; also eats water plants and plankton. Feeds by swimming slowly in an almost vertical position with its mouth extended, sucking up food from mud. Spawns in April–June, collecting in shoals near the surface of shallow, weed-filled water. Young are mature in 3–4 years, and live for up to 20.

Pike
Esox lucius

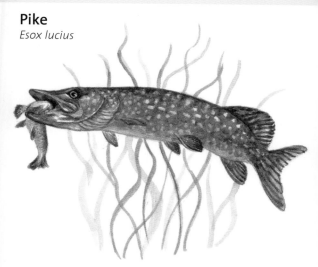

SIZE AND DESCRIPTION Length to 1.7m. Body long and greenish-brown, with golden-green bands and spots; white along the belly. Head broad, with a pointed snout. Name derives from the pole weapon known as a pike.

HABITAT AND DISTRIBUTION Sluggish streams, and weedy ponds, lakes and canals. Found across Europe and in North America.

FOOD AND HABITS Adult Pike are voracious predators, preying on animals of up to half their weight such as invertebrates, fish, frogs, water birds and rodents. They remain stationary in water for long periods, before dashing out to strike their prey with lightning speed. Eggs are laid in February–May in weed-filled shallow water. Lifespan to 30 years, 5–15 years average.

Spined Loach
Cobitis taenia

SIZE AND DESCRIPTION Length to 12cm (f); usually 8–10cm. Elongated and narrow, yellow-brown body with a distinct row of blotches along each side. Six short barbels around the mouth, and a retractable two-pointed spine in a pocket under each eye.

HABITAT AND DISTRIBUTION Densely vegetated mud- or silt-bottomed stagnant ponds, ditches, lakes, slow-flowing rivers and canals. Found from Siberia to Spain; not Scotland, Wales, Ireland and the far north.

FOOD AND HABITS Buries itself in the bed of a water body, leaving only its head and tail exposed. Feeds at night, consuming sand on the bed, and with it small animals and other organic material; ejects the sand through its gills. Spawns in April–June. Lifespan to 10 years in captivity, 3–5 years average.

Crested Newt
Triturus cristatus

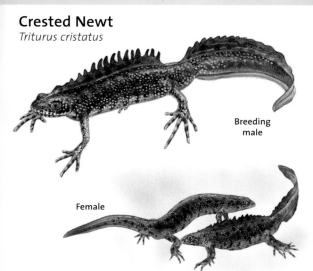

Breeding male

Female

SIZE AND DESCRIPTION Length 11–16cm. Large, colourful and warty. Upperparts dark brown or slaty-black. Underside bright orange-yellow spotted with black. Breeding male develops a ragged crest along the back and another on the tail.

HABITAT AND DISTRIBUTION Breeds in lowland water bodies such as clay pits, reservoirs, ditches and ponds, preferring pools 30–100cm deep. Occurs across Europe except Ireland, Iberia and northern Scandinavia.

FOOD AND HABITS Hunts invertebrates and frog tadpoles at night. Enters the water in mid-March, and remains until July–August. Hibernation begins in October. Eggs are laid on leaves. Larvae metamorphose in four months, and adults are sexually mature at three years. Lifespan up to 27 years.

Common Newt
Triturus vulgaris

Male

SIZE AND DESCRIPTION Length 7–11cm. Centre of male's belly is bright orange or yellow with dark brown patches. Breeding male develops a wavy crest along the neck, back and tail. Smaller female is less clearly marked, lacks a crest and has a paler belly.

HABITAT AND DISTRIBUTION Damp places in many habitats. Found across Europe except the far north and far south.

FOOD AND HABITS Eats insects, caterpillars, crustaceans, molluscs, worms, tadpoles and slugs. Adults enter the water in February–March, leaving it in June–July to hibernate in October. Pairs perform complex displays in the water. Lifespan up to 20 years.

Palmate Newt
Lissotriton helveticus

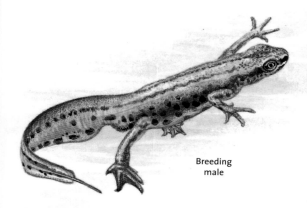

Breeding male

SIZE AND DESCRIPTION Length to 9.5cm. Smooth skin; body pale olive-brown above with small dark spots, and usually a dark streak across the eye. Cream-white or pale orange belly, sometimes with spotting. Breeding male has a low, smooth-edged crest along the back, webbed feet and a filament about 10mm long at the tail tip.

HABITAT AND DISTRIBUTION Ponds, lakes, canals, marshes and sometimes acid pools on upland moorland and in coastal areas. Found in most of western Europe, including Britain.

FOOD AND HABITS Feeds voraciously in ponds, consuming tadpoles and small aquatic insects. Hibernates in November–March under logs and stones. Lifespan usually about 12 years.

Common Frog
Rana temporaria

SIZE AND DESCRIPTION Length 6–8cm. Smoother skin and longer hindlegs than Common Toad's (page 146). Hindlegs are short compared with those of other frogs. Colour and pattern vary. Snout is rounded and the large black eyes are surrounded by gold flecked with brown. Moves with a springing leap.

HABITAT AND DISTRIBUTION Widespread in moist shady habitats, from northern Spain to the North Cape. Absent from Iceland, Orkney and Shetland.

FOOD AND HABITS Snails, slugs, worms, woodlice, beetles and flies are flicked into the wide mouth by its long tongue. Hibernates in pond mud or rotting vegetation on land. Lays up to 1,400 eggs. Tadpoles metamorphose into froglets in 12 weeks, and stay near water until hibernation in October–November. Lifespan up to eight years.

Edible Frog
Rana esculenta

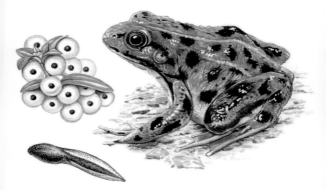

SIZE AND DESCRIPTION Length 5–12cm. Colour ranges from mainly green to mainly brown. Generally a number of dark spots on the back and flanks, with the long back legs often having dark bands. Usually a straw-yellow or lime-green line running along the centre of the back. Underside mottled pale white to yellow and black.

HABITAT AND DISTRIBUTION Highly aquatic and occurs in a variety of waterways. Widespread across much of mainland Europe, and naturalized in Britain.

FOOD AND HABITS Feeds on insects of various kinds. Very active during the day; basks even in the hottest sun. Tadpoles can grow very large (up to 4cm), because they overwinter, metamorphosing into frogs in the following spring.

European Tree Frog
Hyla arborea

SIZE AND DESCRIPTION Length 3–6cm. Small and smooth-skinned, long-legged tree frog with disc-shaped adhesive pads on its toes. Largely bright green, rarely yellow or brownish, blue, grey or mottled, with a brownish or blackish line along each side of the body that bends upwards and forms a dark patch just before the back legs. Able to change colour, like chameleons.

HABITAT AND DISTRIBUTION Occurs on trees, bushes and reeds outside the breeding season, and in quiet sunny ponds, ditches and flooded areas during breeding. Widely distributed in Europe, except the far north and south, and introduced very locally in southern Britain.

FOOD AND HABITS Adhesive pads on the toes enable it to clamber about, usually at night, in vegetation, where it feeds mainly on insects and spiders. During the breeding season males give loud rattling calls mainly at night.

Marsh Frog
Rana ridibunda

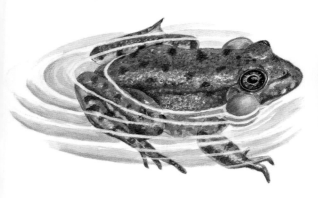

SIZE AND DESCRIPTION Length 5–14cm. Large and strong water frog with a blunt snout and long legs. Upperside is mostly olive-brown to grey, rarely dark green to pale green or yellowish, with irregular dark patches, and often a bright central dorsal line. Underside is whitish with dark patches.

HABITAT AND DISTRIBUTION Favours open areas near still or slow-flowing water bodies, often lakes with sunny and well-vegetated banks, rivers and small temporary pools. Occurs across much of Europe, and introduced to England.

FOOD AND HABITS Feeds on insects, spiders, earthworms and slugs. Crackling call made up of bursts of 'quacking' croaks during the breeding season. These are issued through pouches in males (vocal sacs), shown above on either side of the head. Lays eggs on sub-aquatic vegetation.

Common Toad
Bufo bufo

SIZE AND DESCRIPTION Length 8–15cm. Skin warty and usually orange-brown or olive. Female is larger than male. Walks and hops.

HABITAT AND DISTRIBUTION Lives in a range of habitats, but usually found in damp places. Absent from Ireland, northern Scandinavia and the Mediterranean islands.

FOOD AND HABITS Insects, larvae, spiders, worms and slugs are grabbed by the long and sticky, prehensile tongue. Emerges from hibernation to enter the water in February–March. Hibernates again in October. Male clings to female's back and fertilizes the ribbons of 600–4,000 eggs as she releases them. Toadlets leave ponds in late July–August. Lifespan up to 40 years.

Midwife Toad
Alytes obstetricans

SIZE AND DESCRIPTION Length 4–5.5cm. Small and plump toad with prominent eyes. Skin is warty, with a row of large, mostly red warts that start at the neck and continue to the bases of the hind legs. Upperside is mostly grey, brown or olive, the underside paler.
HABITAT AND DISTRIBUTION Lives in damp areas of gardens, along field edges and in woodland. Found in western Europe, and introduced to several locations in England and Wales.
FOOD AND HABITS Hunts nocturnally for worms, spiders and insects. Often hides under logs or rocks during the day. Males utter high-pitched, musical 'toop toop toop' calls at night. Like most other toads, moves with a shuffling walk or small hops. Male carries fertilized eggs for 6–8 weeks, until they hatch. Tadpoles develop in ponds, puddles or ditches.

Natterjack
Bufo calamita

SIZE AND DESCRIPTION Length 4–9cm. Stocky and rather thickset body, with upperparts brownish, grey, yellowish, olive or greenish, and variable dark patches and reddish warts. Long thin yellow line along the length of the body is a distinguishing feature. Underside is whitish with darker spots.

HABITAT AND DISTRIBUTION Found in western and central Europe. In Britain, where it is very localized, it occurs especially on heathland and in dunes. It favours open, dry and warm places with sand or other light soil that is easy to dig into to make burrows in which to hide during daytime, and where there are pools in which to breed.

FOOD AND HABITS Diet includes beetles, slugs, snails, worms and spiders. Rarely walks or hops, but tends to scurry in short bursts rather like a mouse. Males call frequently with a unique loud rattling voice, usually at night. Eggs are laid in shallow, sunny and sparsely vegetated water bodies, often new and temporary puddles.

Common Lizard
Zootoca vivipara

SIZE AND DESCRIPTION Length 10–16cm. Tail can be more than twice
the body length. Skin has obvious scales and a variable pattern.
Female usually has a stripe down the middle of her back. Pale spots
on the back are more obvious in male than female, and pale
underside is orange in some males. Also called Viviparous Lizard.
HABITAT AND DISTRIBUTION Inhabits a wider range and more northerly
areas than any other reptile species. Found from Ireland and north-
west Spain across Europe and Asia east to Siberia, Sakhalin and
Hokkaido (Japan). Favours moist cool lowland areas, as well as middle
and high altitudes in the Pyrenees and Alps. May be very common in
some habitats, such as gravel pits, embankments, pastures, mountain
meadows, heaths, forest edges and clearings.
FOOD AND HABITS Feeds on small insects, arthropods, centipedes and
isopodes. Hibernates in October–February. Viviparous: the young
hatch from 3–12 transparent eggs within the female's body in
July–September. Lifespan up to 12 years.

Grass Snake
Natrix natrix

SIZE AND DESCRIPTION Length
70–150cm. Female is bigger
than male. Slender pale snake with
a distinct head and dark marks on either side of the neck. Mouth
looks curved.

HABITAT AND DISTRIBUTION Lowland hedgerows, woodland margins,
heaths, moorland, water meadows, gravel pits and gardens. Found in
England and Wales across continental Europe, except the far north
and far south.

FOOD AND HABITS Eats frogs, fish, tadpoles, newts, mice, voles and birds.
Swims well. Hibernates in October–March in holes, crevices or manure
heaps. Mating takes place in April–May; 8–40 eggs are laid in June–
early August in manure heaps, haystacks, compost heaps or rotting
logs. Eggs hatch in August–September. Lifespan up to 25 years.

Mute Swan
Cygnus olor

Adult

Juvenile

SIZE AND DESCRIPTION Length 152cm. Largest flying bird in Britain. Adult is all white, juvenile grey-brown. Orange bill with a black knob at the base (smaller in female) and a graceful curve to the neck.

VOICE Generally silent; hisses when angry or disturbed.

HABITAT AND DISTRIBUTION Almost any still or slow-moving inland water body; also estuaries and sheltered coastal regions. Found across northern and western Europe, and resident in Britain.

FOOD AND HABITS Usually feeds on water by dipping its neck below the surface, sometimes up-ending. Nest is a large mound of plant matter on the edges of water bodies.

Wigeon
Anas penelope

Length 18cm. Drake has a chestnut head with a creamy yellow stripe from the bill over the crown, pinkish breast and short, black-tipped blue bill. White patches on the wings are visible in flight. Drake has a whistling 'whee-oo' call. Winter visitor to much of central and southern Europe, including Britain, often on coastal marshes and estuaries, but also inland. Breeds in the north. Eats mostly plant matter, which it takes from the water's surface. Often seen in flocks grazing on land.

Common Teal
Anas crecca

Length 35cm. Smaller and neater in appearance than Mallard (opposite). Drake has a chestnut head with a green eyestripe, speckled breast and creamy undertail. Drake gives a whistling 'crrick, crrick' call. Found in still or slow-moving fresh water with dense fringing vegetation. Resident in much of Europe. A dabbling duck, eating mostly plants and seeds. May nest some distance from water. Fast in flight; springs up from the water.

Mallard
Anas platyrhynchos

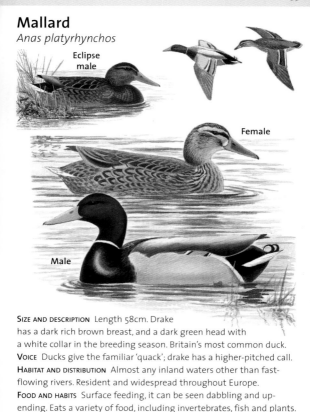

Eclipse male

Female

Male

SIZE AND DESCRIPTION Length 58cm. Drake
has a dark rich brown breast, and a dark green head with
a white collar in the breeding season. Britain's most common duck.
VOICE Ducks give the familiar 'quack'; drake has a higher-pitched call.
HABITAT AND DISTRIBUTION Almost any inland waters other than fast-
flowing rivers. Resident and widespread throughout Europe.
FOOD AND HABITS Surface feeding, it can be seen dabbling and up-
ending. Eats a variety of food, including invertebrates, fish and plants.
Usually nests on the ground under bushes, close to water.

Pochard
Aythya ferina

Female

Male

Length 46cm. Drake
has a chestnut head,
black breast, and grey
back and flanks. Light-blue bill.
Female is brown with a pale
throat. Male gives a soft whistle,
female growls. Inhabits large ponds,
lakes and slow-flowing streams with fringing vegetation. Summer
migrant in northern and eastern Europe, wintering in the south and
west. A diving duck more active at night than during the day, and
often seen resting on the water by day. Nest is a down-lined grass cup
well hidden on the ground.

Goldeneye
Bucephala clangula

Female

Male

Length 46cm. Male is
bright white and black
with a glossy dark green
head that has a circular
white patch below the
eye. Female and juvenile
are grey with a brown
head. In flight, makes a whistling noise with the
wings. Rarely vocal. Male sometimes makes a disyllabic nasal call,
female a harsh growl. Found on coastal and inland waters. Mainly a
winter visitor to Britain, also breeding occasionally in Scotland.
A diving duck. Diet consists mainly of aquatic invertebrates, as well as
amphibians, small fish and some plant material. Nests in the hollows
of mature trees.

Shoveler
Anas clypeata

Female

Eclipse male

Length 51cm. Surface-feeding duck easily recognized by its very large spatulate bill. Drake has a dark green head, white breast and chestnut flanks. Forewing is blue. Drake calls 'took-took'; females 'quack'. Inhabits lakes and reservoirs; favours creeks, reed beds and marshy areas with plenty of cover. Summer visitor to northern and eastern Europe, year-round resident in western Europe and winter visitor to southern Europe. Feeds in shallow muddy water; sieves seeds through its bill. Nest is a down-lined grass cup well hidden on the ground.

Male

Tufted Duck
Aythya fuligula

Female

Length 43cm. A jaunty little diving duck. Drake is black and white with a drooping crest on the back of the head; duck is dark brown with the suggestion of a crest. Bill is blue with a dark tip. Tends to be silent. Inhabits medium-sized or large fresh waters with fringing vegetation. Widespread in Europe, wintering south to the Mediterranean. Dives deeper than Pochard (opposite), eating mostly insects and molluscs. Nests on the ground a few metres from the water's edge.

Male

Little Grebe
Tachybaptus ruficollis

Juvenile

Adult winter

Adult summer

SIZE AND DESCRIPTION Length 27cm. In breeding plumage the cheeks and throat are bright chestnut, the upperparts dark brown. In winter the birds are greyish, but still have the abrupt 'powder-puff' rear. Sexes are similar. Also called Dabchick.

VOICE Whinnying song.

HABITAT AND DISTRIBUTION Still and slow-moving waters from ponds to rivers. Found in much of Europe except the far north.

FOOD AND HABITS Dives for food, mostly small fish. Rather skulking. Nests among waterside vegetation such as rushes, or under overhanging branches.

Great Crested Grebe
Podiceps cristatus

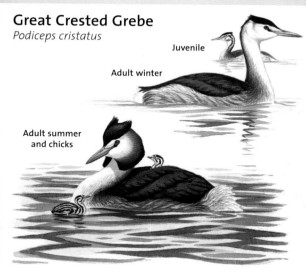

Juvenile

Adult winter

Adult summer
and chicks

SIZE AND DESCRIPTION Length 48cm. Unmistakable in breeding plumage;
both sexes have a large horned crest and ruff, which are lost in winter.
Chicks are striped, with red patches on the neck.

VOICE Generally silent. Call is usually a harsh bark; crooning song.

HABITAT AND DISTRIBUTION Still waters, ponds, lakes and reservoirs, and
slow-flowing rivers. Occurs in much of Europe except the far north.
Following a catastrophic decline in the Victorian era, when the
species' feathers were used to decorate women's hats, populations
have recovered due to strict protection.

FOOD AND HABITS Dives for food, mostly fish and invertebrates, and
some plant matter. Courtship display (page 158) is spectacular. Nests
on a floating mat of water plants near the water's edge.

Grebe Courtship Display

The courtship display of the elegant Great Crested Grebe (page 157)
takes place in February and is spectacular. It includes facing each
other, head shaking and diving under each other (1); turning away
from each other in a bashful manner (2); the female engaging a
'butterfly-like' posture while the male stands erect (3); facing each
other with heads low carrying token nesting material, usually water
weed (4); and finally presenting each other with water weed (5).

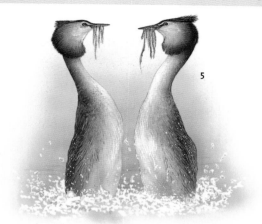

5

Nesting

Bittern
Botaurus stellaris

SIZE AND DESCRIPTION Length 75cm. Plumage is brown marbled and striped with buff and black, offering good camouflage against dead reeds in its habitat. Freezes in an upright position when alarmed.
VOICE In spring male utters a far-carrying booming 'woomb' or 'oo-hoo-oomb', like a foghorn, mainly at night. Call in flight is a barking 'cow'.
HABITAT AND DISTRIBUTION Large freshwater reed beds year-round in much of central Europe. Rarely breeds in Britain, and more widespread in winter.
FOOD AND HABITS Eats fish, frogs, insects, small mammals and birds, and snakes. Hunts by walking slowly, lifting its feet high with each step. Nest is a reed platform among reeds.

Alarm posture

Adult

Grey Heron
Ardea cinerea

SIZE AND DESCRIPTION Length 95cm. Very large and mainly grey, with black-and-white markings. Breeding plumage includes long black plumes on the head. Neck is tucked back in flight; wingbeats are slow and ponderous.

VOICE Flight call is a hoarse, croaking 'kraark' and 'chraa'; bill-clapping at the nest.

HABITAT AND DISTRIBUTION Ponds, marshes, lakes, rivers, canals, flooded fields and estuaries. Occurs across Europe year round.

FOOD AND HABITS Feeds on fish, amphibians, small mammals, insects and reptiles. Hunts by stalking slowly through shallow water, or standing motionless waiting for prey to come within reach, when it strikes with lightning speed. Nests in colonies, usually high in tall trees, in a huge nest.

Typical posture

Juvenile

Adult

Kestrel
Falco tinnunculus

Length 34cm. Distinctive long tail and
pointed wings. Male has a grey head, black-
tipped grey tail and dark-flecked russet
back. Female and juvenile lack the grey
head, and have a brown tail with
narrow bars, and more dark flecks on
the back. Noisy at nest-site; rasping
'kee-kee-kee-kee' call. Breeds in cities and
towns. May be seen flying over gardens,
and inhabits farmland, moorland
and other open areas. Resident
across Europe. Hovers above
grassland or perches on trees and pylons. Also feeds on small birds,
large insects and lizards. Lays eggs in a hole or on a bare ledge.

Male

Female

Hobby
Falco subbuteo

Length 32cm. Dashing little falcon
that looks like a large swift in
flight. Dark slaty-grey above with
dark moustaches on the white
cheeks and throat, and red
thighs. Uses a repeated clear
'kew-kew-kew' call. Found
on heathland and in
woodland. Summer visitor
to Britain. Feeds on small birds and large insects, which are often
eaten in flight. Usually nests in an abandoned crow's nest.

Adult

Juvenile

Water Rail
Rallus aquaticus

SIZE AND DESCRIPTION Length 24cm.
Secretive bird that is often hidden in
reeds and more often heard than seen.
Grey underparts, white-barred flanks, a
red bill and a pointed tail that is usually
held erect.

VOICE Pig-like squeaking and grunting, and a
high-pitched 'kip-kip'. Male display call 'kurp
kurp kurp', female 'tchik-tchik'.

HABITAT AND DISTRIBUTION Reed beds and other
densely vegetated wetland. Widespread in
Europe; summer visitor in the north.

FOOD AND HABITS Omnivorous. Diet
consists mainly of small
animals such as worms,
molluscs, shrimps,
crayfish, spiders, insects,
amphibians and fish;
also feeds on plant
matter. Nest is a
cup of vegetation,
usually on a thick
stand of reeds
or rushes.

Juvenile

Adult

Moorhen
Gallinula chloropus

Length 30cm. Distinctive slaty plumage, dark brown wings, white undertail coverts, yellow-tipped red bill and green legs. Flicks tail as it walks with a careful tread. Juvenile is brown. Calls include harsh, metallic 'krrek' and 'kittick'. Inhabits ponds, rivers, canals, lakes and marshes across Europe. Feeds on seeds, insects, molluscs, leaves and carrion. Nest is a bulky mound of vegetation on the water.

Adult

Juvenile

Coot
Fulica atra

Length 38cm. Mainly black water bird with a white bill and shield on the forehead, greenish legs and a domed back. Chicks are black with rufous heads. Juveniles are greyish. Call usually a loud 'kowk' or variation. Found on still and slow-

Juvenile

Adult

moving fresh water. Dives for food, largely aquatic plants. Often in flocks, especially outside the breeding season. Requires fringing vegetation for nesting. Quarrelsome; fights on the water using its large feet, especially during the breeding season.

Lapwing
Vanellus vanellus

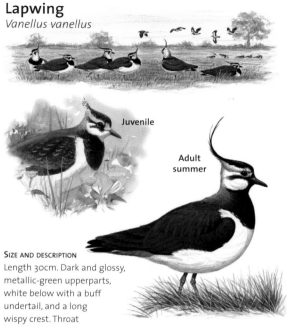

Juvenile

Adult
summer

SIZE AND DESCRIPTION
Length 30cm. Dark and glossy,
metallic-green upperparts,
white below with a buff
undertail, and a long
wispy crest. Throat
black in the breeding season. Juvenile has a short crest. Floppy, loose
and broad-winged flight. Tumbling display flight by males in spring.
VOICE Calls 'peewit'.
HABITAT Farmland, grassland, moorland and marshes; also coasts and
estuaries in winter. Winters in southern and western Europe.
FOOD AND HABITS Diet includes insects, worms and molluscs, with some
vegetable matter. Nests on the ground.

Common Snipe
Gallinago gallinago

Adult

SIZE AND DESCRIPTION
Length 27cm. Wader most
likely to be seen when flushed,
flying off in a zigzag fashion.
Extremely long bill, striped
yellow, and dark brown
head and upperparts.

VOICE
Hoarse cry
when flushed.

HABITAT AND
DISTRIBUTION
Breeds on flood meadows and moors, and winters on
marshes and wetlands in southern and western Europe.

FOOD AND HABITS
Eats mainly worms, as well as molluscs, insects and
other invertebrates. Display flight involves a 45-degree dive, with a
bleating noise caused by air rushing through outspread tail feathers.
Nest is a deep cup well hidden in grass.

Jack Snipe
Lymnocryptes minimus

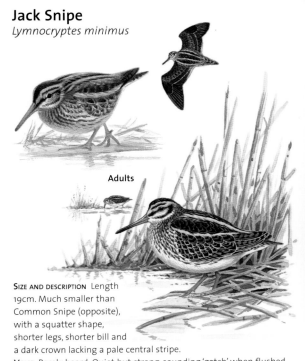

Adults

SIZE AND DESCRIPTION Length 19cm. Much smaller than Common Snipe (opposite), with a squatter shape, shorter legs, shorter bill and a dark crown lacking a pale central stripe.

VOICE Rarely heard. Quiet but strong-sounding 'gatch' when flushed.

HABITAT AND DISTRIBUTION Breeds on moors and marshes in the north. Winters in wet meadows in southern and western Europe.

FOOD AND HABITS Feeds on insects, molluscs, worms and plant material, especially seeds. Habit of bobbing up and down on the spot.

Green Sandpiper
Tringa ochropus

Length 22cm. Distinctly contrasting plumage: upperparts are very dark, underparts white with a strongly separated dark breast. Juvenile is more heavily speckled than adults. Flight call 'tluit-uit-uit'; warning call 'tip tip'; song 'tloo-i tlui'. Mainly a passage migrant in northern Europe, with a few wintering in southern Britain. Occurs on all types of water body during migration. Breeds in damp forests near fresh water. Feeds on plant fragments and invertebrates.

Juvenile

Adult summer

Wood Sandpiper
Tringa glareola

Length 20cm. Size and plumage similar to that of Green Sandpiper, but longer legged and more delicate. Upperparts mottled brownish-grey with distinct spotting and clear feather edges. Juvenile slightly darker. Call is a dry 'chiff if if'. Breeds on taiga wetlands, and during migration is found on mudflats and riverbanks in western and southern Europe. Wades in shallow water, feeding on invertebrates and plants.

Juvenile

Adult summer

Common Tern
Sterna hirundo

Length 35cm. Grey
upperparts, a black crown,
and dark red legs and bill,
which has a black tip. Long
forked tail. White forehead in winter. Call
is a strident 'keeyah' and 'wik-kik-kik'. Breeds
on islands and inshore waters near low-lying
coasts and gravel pits. On passage occurs on lakes and inland waters.
Mostly a summer visitor, wintering outside Europe. Eats fish, worms,
insects, molluscs and crustaceans. Often dives for fish.

Juvenile

Adult
summer

Black-headed Gull
Chroicocephalus ridibundus

Length 37cm. In winter the head is
white with a grey-brown crescent
behind the eye. Breeding birds
have a chocolate-brown head. Bill
is red and finer than the bills of
most other European gulls. Noisy
when in flocks. Calls include a
strident 'kee-yah'. Breeds in colonies
on moorland bogs, freshwater
marshes and lakes, and in reed beds
across northern Europe. In winter
common on ploughed fields and
coasts, and in town parks. Feeds
on seeds and invertebrates, and
scavenges in rubbish.

Adult
summer

Adult
winter

Kingfisher
Alcedo atthis

Adult

Juveniles

SIZE AND DESCRIPTION Length 18cm. Although brightly coloured, Kingfishers are well camouflaged when perched among leaves. Bill is black, but female has a reddish base to the lower mandible. Juvenile has a pale spot at the tip of the bill.

VOICE Distinctive whistle, 'tee-eee' and 'tsee'.

HABITAT AND DISTRIBUTION Rivers, streams and lakes. Visits garden ponds to take small ornamental fish.

FOOD AND HABITS Fish are the main food. Hunts by diving into water from a perch, or by hovering and then diving. Excavates breeding tunnels in steep sandbanks.

Swallow
Hirundo rustica

Juvenile

Male

SIZE AND DESCRIPTION Length 19cm, including tail of 3–6.5cm. Wings are long and pointed, the tail deeply forked. Pale cream underparts, dark blue wings and back, and a red throat with a blue-black neck band.

VOICE High-pitched 'vit-vit' call in flight. Warning call for cats and other ground predators is a sharp 'sifflit'; for birds of prey, 'flitt-flitt'. Song is a rapid rattling twitter.

HABITAT AND DISTRIBUTION Summer visitor to northern Europe. Often seen near water. Breeds in farmyards and small-village gardens with surrounding open country.

FOOD AND HABITS Feeds on insects, which it catches in flight by flying low over fields and water. Fast flight with powerful wingbeats. Cup-shaped clay nest is built in buildings.

House Martin
Delichon urbica

Length 12.5cm. Stubby appearance. Rump white; wings, head and tail dark blue. Voice is a harsh twitter that is higher and more drawn-out when agitated, song a series of formless chirps. Summer visitor and migrant across Europe. Breeds in colonies. Rarely seen on the ground, except when collecting mud for nest-building.

Juvenile

Adult

Sand Martin
Riparia riparia

Length 12cm. Small brown bird with white underparts, a brown breast-band and a short forked tail. Twittering song, less musical than Swallow's. Summer visitor and migrant across Europe, inhabiting open country with fresh water. Eats insects such as midges caught in flight. Nests colonially in burrows excavated in sandbanks. On migration may roost in large numbers in reed beds.

Adults

Grey Wagtail
Motacilla cinerea

SIZE AND DESCRIPTION Length 19cm. Longest tailed of European wagtails. Grey above and lemon yellow below, with colour particularly strong under the tail, and pink legs. Summer adult male (shown above) has a distinctive black throat. Tail is constantly wagging.

VOICE Call a sharp 'tzit'. Song a simple and metallic 'ziss-ziss-ziss'.

HABITAT AND DISTRIBUTION Always in the vicinity of water. Occurs year-round in much of Europe; summer visitor to the north and north-east.

FOOD AND HABITS Insectivorous; often chases insects over water. Nest is a grassy cup usually hidden in a cavity near water.

Pied Wagtail
Motacilla alba

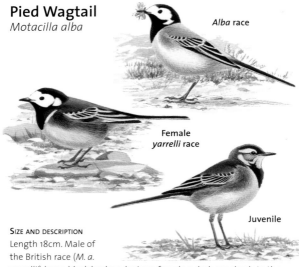

Alba race

Female
yarrelli race

Juvenile

SIZE AND DESCRIPTION
Length 18cm. Male of
the British race (*M. a.
yarrellii*) has a black back and wings, female a dark grey back. In the
continental race (*M. a. alba*), both the male and female have a pale
grey back. In flight, which is undulating, faint double wingbars
can be seen.

VOICE Flight call a 'chissick', sometimes a 'chissick-ick'. Song plain
and twittery.

HABITAT AND DISTRIBUTION Breeds across Britain, often near water, and is
found in towns, gardens and open habitats.

FOOD AND HABITS Runs rapidly after flying insects. On the ground its
gait is rapid, and its head is moved backwards and forwards while
wagging its tail. Prefers feeding on lawns, roofs and roads, and in car
parks, where prey is easily spotted. Nest is a grassy cup in a cavity.

Yellow Wagtail
Motacilla flava

Male *flava* race

Male *thunbergi* race

Juvenile

Female

Male *flavissima* race

SIZE AND DESCRIPTION Length 16cm. Several subspecies, with Yellow (*M. f. flavissima*) by far the most common in Britain. Head green with a yellow throat and supercilium; mantle a brighter yellow-green; slender black legs. Blue-headed (*M. f. flava*) male has a pale blue head. Grey-headed (*M.f. thunbergi*) has a dark grey head.
VOICE Call a rich 'tseep'. Song a simple scratching 'sri'srit sri...'
HABITAT AND DISTRIBUTION Marshes, farmland and meadows, breeding near water. Yellow race breeds in Britain and on neighbouring European coasts. Blue-headed occurs on much of the Continent. Grey-headed breeds in north-east Europe. Winters in Africa.
FOOD AND HABITS Insectivorous. Grassy cup nest is well concealed on the ground.

Bearded Tit
Panurus biarmicus

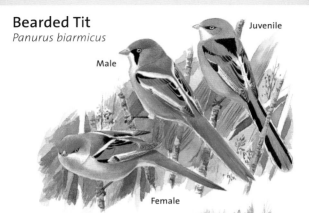

Male

Juvenile

Female

SIZE AND DESCRIPTION Length 15cm.
Tit-like with a plump body and
very long and broad tail. Both
sexes have rich orange-brown
plumage, and male also has
a grey head and black
moustaches. Juvenile streakier
than both male and female,
with dark outer tail feathers.

VOICE Call like tiny bells, a ringing
'ching ching'. Song a softly chirping
'tship tship tshir'.

HABITAT AND DISTRIBUTION Favours reed beds. In Britain quite common in
south-east England.

FOOD AND HABITS Feeds on insects, and reed seeds in winter. Shuffles up
and down reed stems. Builds an open nest of stems in reed beds.

Reed Warbler
Acrocephalus scirpaceus

Length 13cm. Small olive-brown
warbler with a slight rufous tinge to
its upperparts. Buff-coloured below.
Rounded tail. Sexes look similar.
Monotonous churring song. Summer
visitor to Britain, inhabiting mainly reed
beds. Eats water insects. In autumn
feeds on berries, which provide
energy for its long migratory
flight. Builds a nest of woven
grasses slung between reed stems.

Adults

Sedge Warbler
Acrocephalus schoenobaenus

Length 13cm. Olive-brown, streaked-backed warbler with
a rounded tail and rufous-coloured rump. Conspicuous
creamy-white stripe above the eye. Sexes look
similar. Loud, jumbly and scratchy song.
Summer visitor to Britain, migrating to
Africa in late summer. Inhabits
waterside vegetation near
reed beds, rivers and
lakes, and lowland
marshes; also dry
scrubby areas.
Mainly eats insects;
takes berries in
autumn. Nests in
rank vegetation.

Male

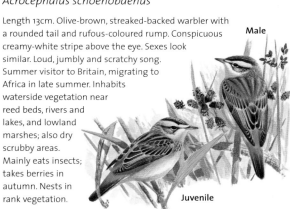

Juvenile

Marsh Tit
Poecile palustris

Length 12cm. Similar to Willow Tit, with a large-headed and short-tailed appearance, but with a shiny black cap, smaller black bib and uniform wings. Call is 'pitchiuu', song a liquid bubbling sound. Found mainly in deciduous woodland, sometimes in gardens, across much of central and western Europe. Diet is mainly insects, with seeds, berries and beechmast. Nests in tree holes, especially in alders and willows.

Adults

Willow Tit
Poecile montanus

Length 12cm. Plumage similar to Marsh Tit's, but Willow has a heavier neck, duller black crown, slightly larger bib and sometimes a pale patch on the closed wing. Call variable, for example a low-pitched, nasal and down-slurred 'zur' or 'si-si-zur zur zur'. Song is a melanchonic and bell-like 'tyu tyu tyu'. Found in forests, scrub and parks in Europe apart from the south-west. Feeds on insects, caterpillars and seeds. Nests in tree hollows, which it excavates itself.

Adults

Reed Bunting
Emberiza schoeniclus

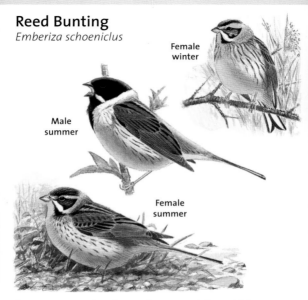

Female
winter

Male
summer

Female
summer

SIZE AND DESCRIPTION Length 15cm. Summer male has a rich brown back streaked darker, grey-brown rump, blackish tail with white outer feathers and whitish upperparts. Crown and face are black, with a white collar running into white moustachial streaks; throat and upper breast are also black. Winter male, female and juvenile are less boldly marked.

VOICE Call is 'tsee-you', song a repetitive 'tsit tsit tsrit tsrelitt'.

HABITAT AND DISTRIBUTION Marshes, scrub and farmland in Europe.

FOOD AND HABITS Feeds mainly on seeds. Often perches on reed stems or telegraph wires. Nest is a grassy cup concealed low in vegetation.

Water Shrew
Neomys fodiens

SIZE AND DESCRIPTION Length 7–10cm (body); 5–7cm (tail). Different from all other British shrews in that it has black fur on its back, is larger, and swims and dives. Often has a small tuft of white hairs on the ears and white hairs around the eyes. Underside is usually silvery-grey.
HABITAT AND DISTRIBUTION Lives along the banks of clear, fast-flowing and unpolluted rivers and streams, as well as around ponds, lakes, canals, marshes, bogs and man-made habitats including gardens. Widely distributed across Europe and Asia.
FOOD AND HABITS Eats a wide variety of terrestrial and aquatic invertebrates and vertebrates, foraging on land and underwater. Lifespan 14–19 months.

European Water Vole
Arvicola amphibius

SIZE AND DESCRIPTION Length 14–22cm (body); 6–7cm (tail). Largest British vole. Brown or black fur, a round body, a chubby face with small protuberant eyes, a hairy tail and ears just extending beyond the fur.

HABITAT AND DISTRIBUTION In Britain found within 2m of the water's edge, along the vegetated banks of ponds, ditches, rivers, streams and marshes. Widespread in much of Europe. Has experienced severe decline in Britain, attributed partly to the introduction of American Mink (page 189) and to habitat destruction; now legally protected.

FOOD AND HABITS Eats mainly vegetation such as grasses, reeds and sedges. Lives in burrows excavated in the banks of ponds, ditches, and slow-flowing rivers and streams. Lifespan usually less than two years.

Whiskered Bat
Myotis mystacinus

SIZE AND DESCRIPTION Length 3–5cm; wingspan 20–25cm. Similar to Daubenton's Bat (opposite), distinguished by its small feet, shaggy dorsal fur and darker face. Upper fur is dark or reddish-brown with golden tips, under fur light greyish-brown. Adults often have pronounced yellowish-brown fur around the neck.

HABITAT AND DISTRIBUTION Inhabits woodland in most of Europe. Often occurs around water and human habitation.

FOOD AND HABITS Feeds on insects and arachnids, foraging in wooded country, often near water. Summer roosts are mostly in buildings, and more rarely in trees. Hibernates in disused mines and caves. Lifespan up to 20 years.

Daubenton's Bat
Myotis daubentoni

SIZE AND DESCRIPTION Length 4.5–5.5cm; wingspan 24–28cm. Fluffy brownish-grey fur on the back, silvery-grey on the underside. Reddish-pink face and nose, and bare area around the eyes.

HABITAT AND DISTRIBUTION Mostly woodland close to still or slow-moving water. Found across Europe, including Britain.

FOOD AND HABITS Insectivorous, emerging at twilight to hunt over water by echolocation for insects such as midges, mayflies and moths. Uses its large hind feet to snatch prey from the surface of the water. Colonies are formed near water, in underground caves, tunnels, cellars and mines, and underneath bridges. Lifespan up to 20 years.

Noctule
Nyctalus noctula

SIZE AND DESCRIPTION Length 3–8cm; wingspan 32–40cm. Coat is golden-brown, but moults into a duller, paler brown in August–September. Narrow wings are dark brown or black.

HABITAT AND DISTRIBUTION Lowland deciduous woodland, parkland and gardens with mature trees. Absent from Iceland, Scotland and the far north.

FOOD AND HABITS Uses tree-holes as summer roosts; also bat boxes. In winter roosts in trees and buildings. Emerges from roosts at dusk. Catches and eats flying insects on the wing over water and pasture near woodland, and in brightly lit areas. Lifespan up to 12 years.

Natterer's Bat
Myotis nattereri

SIZE AND DESCRIPTION Length 4–5cm; wingspan 25–30cm. Long and fluffy fur with dark grey bases to the hairs; conspicuous fringe of hairs along the edge of the tail membrane; long ears that are pink at the bases and darker at the tips; pinkish limbs and a bare pink face. Upper fur is light brown, under fur white or very light buff.

HABITAT AND DISTRIBUTION Open woodland, parkland, hedgerows and areas along waterside vegetation. Occurs across Europe, but not common anywhere.

FOOD AND HABITS Feeds on insects and arachnids caught and eaten both in flight and gleaned off foliage. Hunts over water as well as among trees. Roosts in summer under bridges, and in buildings and hollow trees; hibernates in caves. Lifespan up to 17 years.

Common Pipistrelle
Pipistrellus pipistrellus

SIZE AND DESCRIPTION Length 3.5–4.9cm; wingspan 27–30cm. Soft reddish coat, though the colour may vary. Rounded head with small triangular ears.

HABITAT AND DISTRIBUTION Widespread in a broad range of habitats, including lakes and rivers, unimproved grassland and improved cattle pasture. Found across Europe except the far north.

FOOD AND HABITS Hunts flying insects on the wing. Fast and jerky flight. In summer roosts in buildings, squeezing through tiny gaps to gain entrance. In winter uses buildings and natural sites for hibernation. Usually emerges after sunset, but may be seen during daylight. Average lifespan four years, although recorded living to more than 16.

Barbastelle
Barbastella barbastellus

Size and description Length 4–5cm; wingspan 25–28cm. Blackish fur on the back, with tips of the hairs pale cream or yellow, giving a frosted appearance. Underparts are grey-brown. Ears are black, short, broad and almost meet on the forehead, and the face is squat and pug-like.
Habitat and distribution Occurs across Europe, except the far north and south, in largely wooded riverine habitats. In Britain probably restricted to England and Wales. Threats include the decline of woodland, resulting in the loss of feeding areas and hollow trees for roosting.
Food and habits Heavily reliant on small moths, though it eats other insects and arachnids in winter. Hunts in early dusk low over water and at tree-top height along woodland edges and gardens. Lifespan up to 22 years.

Eurasian Otter
Lutra lutra

SIZE AND DESCRIPTION Length to 84cm (body); 48cm (tail).
Streamlined mustelid whose body is adapted to an
aquatic lifestyle. Water-resistant fur is dense,
consisting of short hairs and longer paler guard hairs.
Feet are webbed, and the tail is long and powerful.
Upperparts are dark brown, chin and upper throat paler, and
underparts markedly paler.
HABITAT AND DISTRIBUTION Wetlands, coastal areas and rivers. Globally
endangered. Once found across Europe, but became extinct in many
areas. Now protected and expanding in Britain.
FOOD AND HABITS Diet includes fish, other small vertebrates and
crustaceans. Active by night in most of its range, but diurnal in
Shetland. Nests in a burrow (holt). Lifespan to 17 years.

American Mink
Mustela vison

SIZE AND DESCRIPTION Length to 40cm (body); 19cm (tail). Semi-aquatic, dark chocolate-brown mustelid, usually with a white chin patch, and white patches on the chest and belly. Tail is slightly bushy. Much smaller than Eurasian Otter (opposite).

HABITAT AND DISTRIBUTION Associated with aquatic habitats. Native to North America, but feral populations associated with the fur trade are now established in much of Europe, including Britain.

FOOD AND HABITS Predator taking a wide variety of prey, including mammals, birds, fish and invertebrates. May have exploited a niche that was not fully occupied by a low otter population, and has declined since much larger otters have started to recolonize Britain. Implicated in catastrophic falls in European Water Vole (page 181) populations in some areas.

Index

192 Index